The
MOTHER AND SON
PRAYER JOURNAL

A Keepsake Devotional
to Share and Connect
through God

CHRISTIE THOMAS

Published in the US by:
ULYSSES PRESS
PO Box 3440
Berkeley, CA 94703
www.ulyssespress.com

ISBN: 978-1-64604-170-1
Library of Congress Control Number: 2020946979

Printed in the United States by Bang Printing
10 9 8 7 6 5 4 3 2 1

Acquisitions editor: Casie Vogel
Managing editor: Claire Chun
Editor: Anne Healey
Proofreader: Kathy Kaiser
Front cover design: Ashley Prine
Cover art: © Marish/shutterstock.com
Interior design: whatdesign @ whatweb.com

CONTENTS

INTRODUCTION

Acts 13:22 says, "And when he had removed him, he raised up David to be their king, of whom he testified and said, 'I have found in David the son of Jesse a man after my heart, who will do all my will.'"

As your son's mom, you have more influence on his faith than anyone else in his life. This is both exciting and a little daunting. How can you, as a woman, raise your son to be a man after God's heart?

These 52 devotions and prayer journal prompts will help you explore what it looks like to be a God-chaser like King David.

Each devotion begins with a fun, relationship-building discussion question and ends with a prayer prompt your son will actually enjoy doing, even if he doesn't like writing. He will doodle his prayers, make lists, write his prayers into comic strip form, and more. There is also space for you to write a prayer for your son based on the day's theme.

This one-of-a-kind journal is for the mother and son who want to connect with each other and with God at the same time. It will be a keepsake of the moments you shared and of your son's responses to God's word. *The Mother and Son Prayer Journal* will deepen your relationship with each other and help you both become God-chasers like David.

How to Keep This Book from Gathering Dust on Your Shelf

We've all done it. We've bought a devotional book or journal with the best of intentions, then discovered it years later at a dust bunny convention under the bed.

Research shows that the best way to start a new habit is to connect it to something we already do in our lives.

If you want to actually use this book (and I assume you do, because you're reading it), you'll need to build it into your day or your week by connecting it to something you already do. There are 52 devotions, meaning you could do one each week for a year. What activity do you already do once per week? You could read your weekly devotion at lunchtime on Saturday, during breakfast on Sunday, or after music lessons. Make sure to pick something you do every week! If you want to use the book faster, pair the devotions with something you do every day instead.

The last element of a good habit is celebration. No, I don't mean going out for ice cream when you finish the book. By "celebration," I mean giving your son a high five or doing a little happy dance when you finish your prayer time. Essentially, you want to do whatever makes you immediately feel *great*. When we feel great about something, we naturally want to do it again!

Write down your habit "recipe" here:
Before/After/During (*current habit*)

....

....

I will use this prayer journal with my son.
Then I will (*celebratory action*)!

....

....

How to Use This Book

1. Focus Verses

At the beginning of each devotion I list the verses I used as the basis for that devotion. In many cases I have woven passages from the English Standard Version of the Bible into the devotion. You can decide whether you want to look up and pre-read the focus verses with your son or simply read the devotion. If you find it too much to read everything, save the focus verses for the times you want to learn more about the passage. It's great to ask the question, "Is that *really* in the Bible?" Then go look it up and find out for yourselves!

2. Ask Each Other

This section provides a discussion question that gently introduces the theme of the devotion. You both get to *ask* the question, and you both get to *answer* the question. This will get you talking about not only the theme but also yourselves. You may be surprised by what you learn about each other!

3. Devotion

Read it out loud together. Reading to your child (even when he can read on his own) has enormous educational and relational benefits. You will probably find that sections you read together will show up in your daily life, giving you an extra chance to nurture his faith.

4. Prayer Section

If your son doesn't love to write, this part may be a little tricky. As a mom, I know that it's possible for me to put so much pressure on my son to write a legible prayer that it could suck the fun out of this journal faster than bleach could remove the dye from a black shirt.

The time you spend on the journal with your son shouldn't feel like school. Make it fun! The great news is that God doesn't need long, deep prayers. He loves to hear from our boys no matter what. Also, drawing a picture counts as a prayer just as much as writing it out does. I have three sons of different ages and writing abilities. When we get to the prayer sections, they can write, draw a picture, or dictate their prayer to me.

Suggestions for a child who doesn't like to write:

- Use fun writing tools. Colorful gel pens help!

- Ask your son to write in list form, or just write a word or two. You could even go so far as to *forbid* him to write in full sentences and see where that kind of reverse psychology takes you.

- Allow him to dictate his answers to you while you write.

- Have him draw his answers. You can even turn an answer into a comic strip with multiple frames.

5. Mother's Prayer Section

You can write as much or as little as you want! Write it while you're with your son, or take time during the week to write out a longer prayer on your own time. This is *your* space. After writing your prayer, be sure to share it with your son so he knows that you're actively praying for him. Pour out your heart to God, and watch as he changes both of you!

Love,
Christie

Ask each other: What makes someone a hero? What makes them great?

Thousands of years ago, a young hero named Alexander built an army and conquered a huge amount of land. He created the biggest empire the world had ever seen. Alexander named 70 cities after himself (which would make writing a letter to someone in Alexandria a bit confusing) and one city after his horse! People called him Alexander the Great because he had taken over so much land. He even told people he was the son of the Greek god Zeus.

Was Alexander really great? Well, that depends on your definition of *great*.

The Bible teaches that true greatness isn't about how much you own or how many people you lead. The greatest king in the Bible was David, and God called him "a man after my heart" (Acts 13:22).

That doesn't mean David was trying to grab God's heart (that sounds squishy) but rather that he was a God-chaser.

Alexander chased power but David chased God. This is what makes someone great, according to God.

Alexander chased power, and when he died at age 32, his empire was divided up and eventually fell apart. David chased God, and God promised that he would have an everlasting kingdom!

Alexander pretended to be the son of a god. David got to be the great-great (and many more greats) grandfather of the actual Son of God, Jesus.

There are a lot of things we can chase, like winning at the science fair, being the best on a sports team, doing the coolest bike tricks, or getting to the top level of a video game.

None of those things are bad. David was also an amazing soldier, leader, and friend, and his people even wrote songs about how cool he was. But he didn't chase fame, money, or power. He chased God.

(What does it look like to chase God? Keep reading this book and we'll find out together!)

Write God a letter (or draw him a picture) about what you are chasing. (What is most important to you right now?) Then pray, "God, please help me want to chase you."

Mother's Prayer Section

2 LOOKING AT THE HEART

1 Samuel 16:1–13

Ask each other: What do you see when you look at me?

When you meet someone new, what's the first thing you notice about them? The style of their hair or clothes? Their laugh or how well they kick a soccer ball?

Let's talk about the time the prophet Samuel got a big lesson about judging people by their outsides. Saul was already the king of Israel, but he had disobeyed God in some big ways, so God told Samuel to anoint a new king in secret.

God could have told Samuel exactly who was going to be the next king, but instead, he just told him which family to visit. Samuel obediently walked over to Bethlehem to meet Jesse's family.

When he got there, Jesse's oldest son, Eliab, walked past him. Samuel thought, "*Wow*. Now *that* guy would make a great king!"

The Bible doesn't tell us why Samuel thought that, so what do *you* think?

Maybe Eliab was super strong, with muscles on top of muscles. Maybe he was the tallest guy around. Maybe his beard was the bushiest. All we know is what God told Samuel next:

> But the Lord said to Samuel, "Do not look on his appearance
> or on the height of his stature, because I have rejected him.
> For the Lord sees not as man sees: man looks on the outward
> appearance, but the Lord looks on the heart." (1 Samuel 16:7)

OK, apparently Eliab wasn't going to be the next king. In fact, Jesse went on to present seven sons to Samuel, but God didn't pick any of them! It didn't matter if they were the smartest or the strongest or the fastest, because God wasn't looking for those things.

Finally, Samuel scratched his head. Could he have heard God wrong? Where was the next king?

"Are all your sons here?" he asked Jesse. No, Jesse's youngest son was taking care of the sheep. They sent someone to get him. When he got there, God told Samuel that *this* was the king: the youngest kid in the family, who got stuck with the dirty work.

Samuel picked up his flask of oil and poured it over the head of the new king, the one who had the best heart. David.

Pray: "God, what do you see when you look at me? Please show me."

You might have to be quiet for a minute or two after you pray, but wait for God to give you the ideas. Then write down whatever you think of, even if it's just one word.

....

....

....

....

Mother's Prayer Section

....

....

....

....

....

3 THE HOLY SPIRIT
1 Samuel 16:13

Ask each other: What's the biggest storm you remember?

Have you ever been in a huge windstorm? Trees bend nearly sideways, dust whips down the street, and even high-rise buildings sway in the wind. Big windstorms can cause a lot of damage when they knock down trees or become whirling tornadoes.

Now imagine being outside on a perfect summer day. You lie in a field, and the grass rustles gently in the breeze. An eagle soars high above.

Where would you rather be? If you chose the gentle wind, you're not alone! But would it surprise you to know that sometimes good things can come from the craziest windstorms? Dust storms in the Sahara desert in Africa send beneficial minerals all the way to the Amazon rainforest in South America, and these minerals help the rainforest grow.

In the Bible, the Holy Spirit is sometimes described as a wind, but we don't really know what form the Holy Spirit took for David when Samuel anointed him. All we know is this:

Then Samuel took the horn of oil and anointed him in the midst of his brothers. And the Spirit of the Lord rushed upon David from that day forward. (1 Samuel 16:13)

Sometimes the Holy Spirit would help him do amazing, powerful things that changed his country, like a crazy windstorm making his enemies shiver. Other times, the Holy Spirit helped him write poetry and sing songs to God that we still sing today, like grass rustling on a warm day.

Having the Spirit of the Lord upon him did not make David's life easy. In fact, it took about 15 years for David to actually become king after he was anointed by Samuel! David spent most of those years in battles or hiding.

Most people in the Old Testament didn't actually receive the Holy Spirit. Only super special people got the Holy Spirit's help, and they got it only for specific jobs, like speaking prophecies or fighting an enemy.

The good news is that when Jesus left, he sent the Holy Spirit to be in every single believer. That means you! The same Holy Spirit that helped David be courageous and wise is in you. Forever.

Sometimes the Holy Spirit might be in you like a windstorm, helping you change the world. But most times, the Spirit is like a gentle breeze. He whispers through your mind and heart, teaching you and helping you become a God-chaser.

Draw a comic of the Holy Spirit coming to you. What do you say to the Holy Spirit?

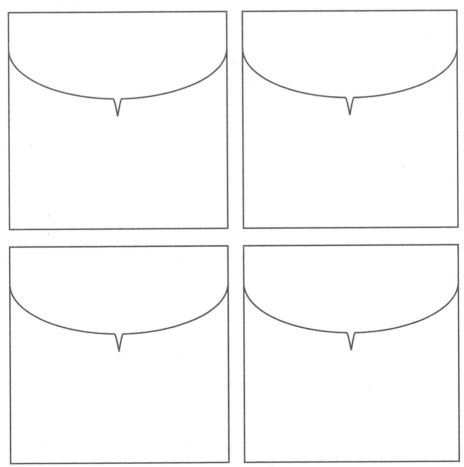

Mother's Prayer Section

4 COMFORT FROM GOD
1 Samuel 16:14-23

Ask each other: What makes you feel better
when you're having a bad day?

Samuel anointed David in secret because he knew that Saul would probably try to kill David if he knew. But God didn't hide David away; instead, he plopped him right under Saul's nose!

Saul had shown that he didn't truly want to follow God, so God placed his Spirit on David and left Saul. The Bible says a harmful spirit tormented Saul. We don't know exactly what that was—maybe an evil spirit or maybe a form of mental illness, or maybe Saul simply understood that God's Spirit had left him.

When you're having a bad day, maybe you go play outside or hide under your blanket for a while. Saul's attendants decided he needed to put on some music! They looked for someone who could play the lyre (a stringed instrument like a harp) to make Saul feel better.

> One of Saul's servants said, "Behold, I have seen a son of Jesse the Bethlehemite, who is skillful in playing, a man of valor, a man of war, prudent in speech, and a man of good presence, and the Lord is with him." (1 Samuel 16:18)

Which son of Jesse do you suppose this was? I'll give you one guess. Yes, it was David!

> And Jesse took a donkey laden with bread and a skin of wine and a young goat and sent them by David his son to Saul. And David came to Saul and entered his service. And Saul loved him greatly, and he became his armor-bearer. (1 Samuel 16:20-21)

Doesn't God have a great sense of humor? Who would have guessed that this would be a good place for a hidden, future king! But it gave David a chance to watch a king do his job. It was like job training, except that Saul didn't realize he was training David!

While David was watching and learning, he was also able to help Saul. David's playing was full of God's Spirit, and it soothed the Spirit-less Saul.

Not only did David play the lyre, but he also wrote music. Many of his songs were saved and written down in the Bible. They're called psalms. We're going to look at some of them together, because God uses many of them to comfort us, just like he used David's music to comfort Saul.

Write or draw a note to God about what makes you feel better when you're having a bad day.

Mother's Prayer Section

5 GOD'S HAND OF BLESSING
Psalm 139:1-12

Say to each other: Tell me about a time you
tried to hide from your parent(s).

You've heard of Santa Claus and his elves, right? According to the story, they watch over children day and night in order to put each child on the naughty or nice list. A naughty kid is supposed to get coal in their stocking on Christmas, and of course, a nice kid receives a gift.

Lots of people think that God is just like Santa, watching how we behave in order to punish us or give us gifts. But is that true?

Here's what David wrote about God:

O Lord, you have searched me and known me!
You know when I sit down and when I rise up;
you discern my thoughts from afar.
(Psalm 139:1–2)

Hmm, God does sound a bit like Santa Claus here, doesn't he? It sounds like he's watching you through the window with high-powered binoculars and reading your mind! But God isn't a creepy peeper; he's a good God who loves his people. We know that because David kept writing, and he said this:

You hem me in, behind and before,
and lay your hand upon me.
(Psalm 139:5)

Imagine God placing his hand on your head. How does it feel? Another Bible translation calls it "your hand of blessing" (New Living Translation). I'm glad it's a hand of blessing and not one of punishment, because the rest of Psalm 139 says that we can't ever hide from God!

You couldn't hide from God if you left the Milky Way, went to the bottom of the Mariana Trench, or went into another dimension. Even if you discovered a place where not a single particle of light could get in, God would still see you. That's not something to be afraid of, because God's hand of blessing is on your head!

Here's another way to think about how God watches you: Have you ever wondered if your mom has eyes in the back of her head? It seems like she always knows what you're doing, even when you're trying to keep a sneaky secret. She pays attention to you because she loves you, not because she's trying to ruin your life.

It's the same with God. He watches over you, not to give you a lump of coal if you're bad, but to love you.

What does it feel like to know that God's hand of blessing is on your head? Draw (or write) what that looks like to you.

Mother's Prayer Section

6 FEARFULLY AND WONDERFULLY MADE
Psalm 139:13–18

Ask each other: What is one thing about
yourself that you really like?

Every human being started as a single cell, too small to see except with a microscope. But we change fast!

- Four weeks after being just one cell, you had a little heart, and it started beating.
- By 10 weeks you had fingernails.
- By around 12 weeks you were doing flips and dancing inside your mom's belly. Can you still dance like that?
- If your mom went to the doctor when you were around 14 weeks, the doctor would have been able to use an ultrasound machine to see that you are a boy.

Thousands of years ago, there were no ultrasound machines, so David didn't know these incredible facts. But God showed him that something special had happened as he grew inside his mom. Even before David was born, God knew what would make him laugh, what he would be good at, and even what would scare him.

In Psalm 139, David wrote this about God:

For you formed my inward parts;
you knitted me together in my mother's womb.
I praise you, for I am fearfully and wonderfully made.
Wonderful are your works;
my soul knows it very well.
(Psalm 139:13–14)

David knew that every part of him had always been known to God, even when he was being made in secret, beyond the eyes of humans. God also knew everything about *you* before you were born. He knew what would make you laugh, what you would be good at, and even what would scare you. Let's say with David, "Thank you, God, for making me!"

Maybe you wonder if God made a mistake when he made you. Maybe your body doesn't look like everyone else's, or maybe it doesn't work like everyone else's. Maybe you wish you were better at basketball or reading or talking to people.

You can tell that to God. He's not afraid of you or what you might say. David told God everything, even when he was cranky or whiny or scared. He knew he could trust God with every part of himself.

God knew every part of you before you were born. He knew what special gifts he had buried inside you, waiting to be found. You might not know them yet, but you can know that God's works are always wonderful.

Make a list of the things you like about yourself. Make another list of the things you don't like. Then put your hand on the list and say, "I praise you, for I am fearfully and wonderfully made."

Mother's Prayer Section

7 GOD AS SHEPHERD

Psalm 23

Say to each other: Tell me about an
animal you've taken care of.

David was a shepherd. If you've never been a shepherd, let's take a peek at what that looks like.

We often think that sheep are dumb, but they're actually quite intelligent. Recent scientific studies show that sheep have friends and have feelings, just like us. If you get too close to their young, they will kick you really hard. But we humans like to wear their wool, so we keep them in flocks and try not to get too close to those hooves!

A shepherd cares for his flock of sheep. He leads the sheep to food and water, and keeps them safe from predators by beating them away with a wooden rod. The shepherd also has to watch out for poisonous plants and search for sheep who have wandered off. If a sheep wanders away or gets stuck, the shepherd catches it with his staff, hooking its curled end around the sheep's neck and bringing the sheep back into the flock.

In Psalm 23, David compares God to a shepherd. It's probably the most famous psalm, so let's read the whole thing. Imagine yourself as a sheep and God as a shepherd.

The Lord is my shepherd; I shall not want.
He makes me lie down in green pastures.
He leads me beside still waters.
He restores my soul.
He leads me in paths of righteousness
for his name's sake.
Even though I walk through the valley of the shadow of death,
I will fear no evil,
for you are with me;

your rod and your staff,
they comfort me.
You prepare a table before me
in the presence of my enemies;
you anoint my head with oil;
my cup overflows.
Surely goodness and mercy shall follow me
all the days of my life,
and I shall dwell in the house of the Lord forever.

In this psalm David shows God caring for him and using his rod and staff to protect and guide him.

David used his own experience as a shepherd to understand who God is. You can do that too. Maybe you imagine God to be like a superhero, or a teacher, or a lighthouse. God is like all those things and more. He's incredible!

Write a short psalm, starting with "The Lord is my..."

....

....

....

Mother's Prayer Section

....

....

....

....

8 TRUSTING GOD TO HELP
1 Samuel 17:32–37

Ask each other: What is the most dangerous
thing you've ever done on purpose?

Sometimes humans do crazy things, like lifting up a car to help someone trapped under it, or climbing a wall with barely anything to hold onto.

These amazing things seem like superpowers, but they're made possible by a hormone we all have, called adrenaline. Your body produces adrenaline when you are afraid. It helps extra blood go to your muscles so you can fight or run away. Sometimes people do scary things on purpose in order to feel this rush of adrenaline, because it makes them feel powerful.

In 1 Samuel, we read about a terrifying giant of a man who challenged the Israelites to single combat (a fight between two warriors). David, a teenager, stepped up to fight, but King Saul told him that he was too young. David didn't argue. Instead, he told this story:

Your servant used to keep sheep for his father. And when there came a lion, or a bear, and took a lamb from the flock, I went after him and struck him and delivered it out of his mouth. And if he arose against me, I caught him by his beard and struck him and killed him. (1 Samuel 17:34–35)

It sounds a bit like he's bragging, but David knew he was saved by more than just adrenaline.

He said, "The Lord who delivered me from the paw of the lion and from the paw of the bear will deliver me from the hand of this Philistine" (1 Samuel 17:37).

David knew that he was able to kill the lion and the bear not because he was so strong or smart or had the best weapon, but because God had delivered him.

It wasn't just adrenaline. It was God.

We humans often think we have to do hard things—like passing a tough math test or apologizing to a friend—all by ourselves. If we can't do it, we think, "I just wasn't good enough." If we do well on the test or apologize without peeing our pants, we start to think, "I guess I'm just really good at that."

Neither of those thoughts reflect a God-chaser heart like David's. David knew he could do hard things *because* he had God's help. Even hard things like standing up to a giant.

Tell God about something hard that's in your life right now (write it down or draw it). Ask him for his help.

Mother's Prayer Section

9 SETTING A GOOD EXAMPLE
1 Samuel 17:33

Ask each other: Have you ever been told
you were too little to do something?

Normally, it's great to be a kid. You get to eat candy without worrying about calories, you get to play with friends and not worry about paying bills, and you get recess.

But sometimes you want to do something that kids don't normally do, like drive a car or ride the biggest roller coaster. David was one of those kids. Except that he didn't want to drive a car or ride a roller coaster. He wanted to fight a terrifying, enormous soldier in one-on-one combat.

Unsurprisingly, Saul told David, "You are not able to go against this Philistine to fight with him, for you are but a youth, and he has been a man of war from his youth" (1 Samuel 17:33).

But David knew he could do it, even though he was young. He trusted God. He had seen how God had helped him with smaller things, and now he trusted God with this enormous problem. He didn't need big muscles, because he trusted the God who *invented* big muscles. (Sometimes kids are better at trusting God than adults are.)

In the New Testament, there is a letter that Paul wrote to his young friend Timothy, who was a pastor. Paul knew that some people would say Timothy was too young to lead others. So Paul wrote this:

> *Let no one despise you for your youth, but set the believers an example in speech, in conduct, in love, in faith, in purity. (1 Timothy 4:12)*

This is exactly what David did! He didn't let Saul look down on him or reject him because he was young. But he also didn't scream in Saul's face, "I'm big enough! I can do this! I'll show you!" Instead,

33

he set an example for Saul in the words he spoke, in the way he acted, and in his love, faith, and purity.

You can do that too!

You are young, but the Holy Spirit in you is the same Holy Spirit working in adult Christians. Through God's power, you can set an example by trusting God even when no one else does. You can also set an example through the words you speak, the way you act, how you trust God, and how you love others. You'll definitely need God's help for that. But he gives it willingly—we just have to ask!

Tell God about one of these things (speech, conduct, love, faith, purity) that is hard for you, and ask him to change you so that you can be a godly example.

....

....

....

....

Mother's Prayer Section

....

....

....

....

10 GOD'S ARMOR
1 Samuel 17:38–40

Ask each other: What's the worst fight you've ever been in?

If you know you're heading into a sword fight, you probably want to wear armor, right? That's what all the knights, kings, and soldiers do in the movies. They put on thick padding or chain mail and a metal helmet.

David trusted God to protect him from Goliath, just as God had protected him from a lion and a bear. But it would still make sense to wear armor, right? That's what King Saul thought.

> Then Saul clothed David with his armor. He put a helmet of bronze on his head and clothed him with a coat of mail, and David strapped his sword over his armor. (1 Samuel 17:38–39)

Saul put his own armor on David, and it was so big and heavy that David could barely walk! Can you imagine going out to the fight of your life, wearing a helmet that covered your eyes and chain mail that went down to your knees? You'd be a bit protected, but it wouldn't be long before the enemy would knock you over.

Instead of asking for smaller armor, David did something totally crazy. He said to Saul, "I cannot go with these, for I have not tested them" (1 Samuel 17:39).

Then he took all the armor off!

In the New Testament (Ephesians 6:13–17), Paul talked about a different kind of armor. He called it the Armor of God, which included "the helmet of salvation" and "the breastplate of righteousness" instead of a bronze helmet and chain-mail shirt. Instead of a sword that can chop off a giant's head, he wrote about the sword of the Spirit, which is the word of God.

Even though David lived long before Paul wrote those words, I think he understood that God's armor would protect him better than any bronze or iron. Trusting in God didn't mean he stood there and waited for God to do everything. He still picked up five stones and brought his sling to the battlefield. But he knew his God could do big stuff with David's little weapon.

Make a list of the things or people that keep you safe. Then pray, "God, please help me to trust you to care for me, no matter what happens."

....

....

....

....

Mother's Prayer Section

....

....

....

....

....

....

....

Say to each other: Tell me about a time
you desperately needed help.

When Goliath challenged the Israelites to single combat, King Saul trembled in his boots. As the king, he should have been the one to go fight Goliath. But he trusted only in himself, and he knew he couldn't win against Goliath.

David, however, knew this wasn't his fight. It was God's fight.

You see, ancient people believed that battles were decided by their gods. In the age-old Greek story about the Trojan War, the author shows the Greek gods taking sides. Even though it was the humans who were fighting, the story talks about gods and goddesses manipulating people to make the battle go the way they wanted.

David knew he had the only real, living God on his side. He knew God had helped him before and would help him again, not only against Goliath, but against the whole Philistine army standing behind the huge warrior.

Then David said to the Philistine, "You come to me with a sword and with a spear and with a javelin, but I come to you in the name of the Lord of hosts, the God of the armies of Israel, whom you have defied. This day the Lord will deliver you into my hand, and I will strike you down and cut off your head. And I will give the dead bodies of the host of the Philistines this day to the birds of the air and to the wild beasts of the earth, that all the earth may know that there is a God in Israel, and that all this assembly may know that the Lord saves not with sword and spear. For the battle is the Lord's, and he will give you into our hand." (1 Samuel 17:45–47)

David knew the battle was the Lord's and that he was just doing his part. So he approached the battle-hardened soldier with his staff, a few stones, and a sling. As Goliath moved in for the attack, David pushed a rock into his sling and began to swing it around. He ran toward the vicious, angry warrior and opened his sling to let the rock fly out.

And I think you probably know the end of the story. The rock knocked Goliath out, and David used Goliath's own sword to cut off his head.

Who won the battle? David's God: the living God. How's that for a God worth chasing?

Draw a comic of a time you think you might need God's help, and show how you think he might help you. (Hint: ask God for ideas!)

The battle is the Lord's!

Mother's Prayer Section

Ask each other: Who is your favorite
person to hang out with? Why?

In nature, there are many different kinds of animal relationships that seem like friendships but really aren't. When a barnacle lives on a whale, the whale doesn't even notice the barnacle tagging along for the ride. But when a barnacle attaches to a crab, it causes all kinds of problems.

Have you ever had (or been) a friend like this? Maybe you have a friend who just follows the crowd quietly, or maybe you have a friend who always gets you in trouble or isn't always kind to you.

Another kind of relationship in the wild is called competition. That's when animals compete for the same food, like lions and cheetahs competing for the freshest antelope dinner.

Competition in the wild is completely natural, but it's not a great model for human friendships. David and Jonathan could easily have competed. After all, Jonathan was the son of King Saul and probably expected to be the next king—that is, until he found out that David had been anointed as the next king.

Instead of competing for the kingdom or being jealous of David, Jonathan was loyal to his friend. In fact, the Bible says that "he loved him as his own soul" (1 Samuel 18:3).

That's the very best kind of friendship. In nature, it's called mutualism. An example is the relationship between the clownfish and the sea anemone. The clownfish has special mucus that makes it immune to the sting of the anemone, so the clownfish is protected from predators inside the anemone's waving tentacles. The clownfish lures in other fish looking for a colorful snack, who then get stung and eaten by the anemone.

In Psalm 133:1, David wrote, "How good and pleasant it is when brothers dwell in unity!" I bet he was thinking of his amazing friend Jonathan, who loved him better than a clownfish loves an anemone.

Unity means "two or more people acting as one person." They stick together like clownfish and anemones, each person making life better for the other. And when they disagree, they still choose each other.

Do you have any friendships like this? If you have one, hold onto it because it's hard to find! If not, let's talk to God about that right now.

Tell God about your perfect friend. Write a list of things that make a good friend, or draw a picture of you and your friend playing. Thank God for friendships like Jonathan and David's.

Mother's Prayer Section

Say to each other: Tell me about a time you wanted something that someone else had.

After David killed Goliath, King Saul became suspicious. He already knew that God was going to take the kingdom from him. He didn't know that David had already been anointed, but he knew he should keep a close eye on this new hero.

One day, David strummed his lyre in the king's house. One of his jobs was to make King Saul feel more peaceful with his music. Saul sat with his spear in his hand, which doesn't sound very comfortable, but I guess when you're king, you get to do whatever you want. Suddenly, an evil spirit seized Saul and he hurled his spear at David, trying to pin him to a wall like a bug. So much for a peaceful afternoon! David dashed away even as the spear quivered in the wall.

Why did Saul behave like this? Yes, part of it was that harmful spirit, but he was also jealous. Saul knew that God wasn't with him but was with David. Everything David did was successful, from playing the lyre to killing Philistines. Saul's people danced around David, singing:

Saul has struck down his thousands,
and David his ten thousands.
(1 Samuel 18:7)

This made Saul afraid and angry. Saul wanted to be the hero. He wanted to keep his kingdom. He wanted what David had. Saul became so jealous that he tried to murder his son's best friend!

Jealousy can do some pretty awful things to us.

It's like a black hole inside us that eats up our goodness. James 3:16 says, "For where jealousy and selfish ambition exist, there will be disorder and every vile practice." When I really, really want something that someone else has, it makes me dislike that person.

It makes me think bad things about them. It makes me angry when others are nice to them. That black hole can eat up so much of my goodness that I end up hurting others because I'm so jealous.

Saul's jealousy continued to eat him up inside for the rest of his life.

If you're feeling jealous today, here are three steps that can help you:
1. Tell God about it. Write or draw who you're jealous of.

2. Tell yourself truth from the Bible. Look up one of these and write it down: Proverbs 14:30, Proverbs 23:17–18, or 1 Corinthians 13:4.

....

....

....

....

3. Write, "Thank you God for..." and thank God for giving good things to the other person. This is like opening up the door of your heart to God's light, which will fill that black hole!

....

....

....

Mother's Prayer Section

....

....

....

....

....

....

....

....

14 TRUSTING GOD EVEN WHEN WE DON'T UNDERSTAND

1 Samuel 18:6–29

Ask each other: What's the weirdest thing
you've ever read in the Bible?

There is so much we can learn from the Bible, but one important thing to remember about the Bible is that it was written a very long time ago. David lived about 3,000 years ago! It's hard to imagine so many years, isn't it? Because it's so old, sometimes we'll read a part that makes us scratch our heads.

Remember how Saul was super jealous of all the attention David was getting? He concocted a sneaky plan to get David killed. David had just saved the Israelites from the Philistines, so Saul couldn't just throw him in jail. He had promised that the man who killed Goliath could marry his daughter, so he kept that promise—with a twist.

Saul told David that he could marry his daughter Michal but that he had to pay a bride price. This was something that most ancient cultures did and that some modern cultures still do. A man had to pay his wife's dad in order to marry her.

Saul's price? Kill 100 Philistines and bring back proof. (Want to know what the proof was? Look it up in 1 Samuel 18!)

Saul assumed that David would die trying to fight 100 men. But David turned out to be good at this too, and he actually killed 200 Philistines!

Nowadays, we know that it's wrong to murder 200 people for a wife, right? It probably wasn't even a normal thing for the Israelites. Saul didn't actually want David to marry Michal, he wanted to kill him. But David didn't know that, so he did what Saul asked him to do.

When we read verses like this in the Bible, it can make us ask questions like these:

"Why did David agree to murder people for a wife?"

"Why did Jesus teach us to love our enemies when people in the Old Testament killed their enemies?"

"Does God want *me* to hurt bad people?" (P.S. The answer is a big fat NO.)

You may have some answers to these questions, or you may not. It's good to ask them even if you can't figure out the answers for many years. It shows that you're really taking the Bible seriously and want to understand it.

We might not understand everything we read in the Bible, but we can still trust the God it tells us about. He is good even when it seems like his people aren't.

Do you trust God, even when you don't understand him? Write him a short note telling him why or why not.

....

....

....

....

Mother's Prayer Section

....

....

....

....

Say to each other: Tell me about a time
someone was mean to you.

Have you noticed that kids can be really mean sometimes? They call other kids horrible names, pick on smaller kids, and even hurt each other. Mean kids often grow into mean adults. But even most of the meanest adults wouldn't do what Saul did.

David was Saul's armor bearer, his lyre player, and a commander in his army. David was practically Saul's own son because he was Jonathan's best friend and Michal's husband.

Jonathan knew that Saul wanted to kill David, so he convinced his dad to leave David alone. Saul promised not to kill David.

But Saul broke his promise. One night, he ordered his soldiers to surround David's home. They were to kill him in the morning.

Michal heard about this plan, and she didn't want her new husband to be killed! "So Michal let David down through the window, and he fled away and escaped" (1 Samuel 19:12).

Michal tried to give David extra time to escape by making it look like he was sick in bed.

And when Saul sent messengers to take David, she said, "He is sick." Then Saul sent the messengers to see David, saying, "Bring him up to me in the bed, that I may kill him." (1 Samuel 19:14–15)

Saul was willing to kill a sick man in his own bed!

Good thing David was already gone! Can you imagine how sad, frustrated, and angry David must have felt? He was hated by the man he served. He had to escape alone, running away in the night.

It's really hard to be the one who gets bullied. It's also tough to be the person watching it happen. Have you ever watched someone else get bullied? It's tricky to know what to do because we naturally don't want to get involved. We're afraid of getting hurt. I think we can learn from Jonathan and Michal.

Michal helped David escape from her father, even though Saul could have had her killed for helping David. Jonathan stood up to his dad and told him to stop.

The next time you see someone getting bullied, remember that God helped Michal and Jonathan stand up for David. God can help you too.

Draw a comic of someone getting bullied in your school or community. How will you stand up for the kid getting bullied? Will you ask for God's help?

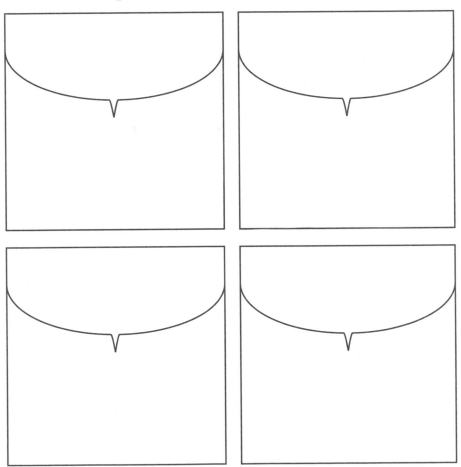

Mother's Prayer Section

....

....

....

....

....

....

....

....

....

....

....

....

....

....

16 BEING TRUTHFUL IN PRAYER
Psalm 59

Ask each other: What, to you, is the
hardest part about praying?

Last time we read that Saul sent men to David's house to kill him, but David's wife helped him sneak away. While David was in hiding, he wrote a prayer that we call Psalm 59.

Let's take a look at it today, because I think you might be surprised at what you're allowed to say to God when you're praying!

Sometimes we think we need to use the right words to talk to God, but he isn't looking for specific words. He just wants to hear from you, no matter what's happening. David didn't even say "please" when he started his prayer! He just told God exactly what he wanted him to do:

Deliver me from my enemies, O my God;
protect me from those who rise up against me;
deliver me from those who work evil,
and save me from bloodthirsty men.
(Psalm 59:1–2)

David reminded God that he was innocent:

For behold, they lie in wait for my life;
fierce men stir up strife against me.
For no transgression or sin of mine, O Lord,
for no fault of mine, they run and make ready.
Awake, come to meet me, and see!
(Psalm 59:3–4)

Did you notice that? David asked God to wake up and pay attention! We know that God is always paying attention, but it can often *feel* like he's not listening. But God isn't mad when we talk to him about our feelings. (He can handle it because he knows the truth!)

You can see that David was still scared, because he said,

Each evening they come back,
howling like dogs
and prowling about the city.
There they are, bellowing with their mouths
with swords in their lips—
for "Who," they think, "will hear us?"
(Psalm 59:6–7)

Even though he was still afraid, David knew that the joke was on them! He wrote that God hears everything and would come to his rescue. Then, even though he wasn't safe yet, David finished his prayer by praising God:

You, O God, are my fortress,
the God who shows me steadfast love.
(Psalm 59:17)

You can rely on God to show you steadfast love too, no matter what is happening in your life.

I think that David was known as a God-chaser partly because he was so honest with God. Let's be honest with God today.

What do you want to tell or ask God?

....

....

....

....

Mother's Prayer Section

Ask each other: What do you do when you're scared?

Have you ever set up a domino line? If you set them up right, you can knock over the first domino and cause other dominos, far away, to fall over. Sometimes this happens in our lives too. When one action causes a whole bunch of other things to happen, we call it the domino effect.

After David snuck away from his house, he started a domino effect. He ran to a nearby town called Nob. It was filled with priests and their families.

David met a priest named Ahimelech. He knew that David was Saul's son-in-law, captain of his bodyguard, and honored in Saul's house, but seeing him without other soldiers around made Ahimelech afraid.

David was also afraid, so he lied. He told Ahimelech that Saul had sent him on a secret mission.

Ahimelech gave him some bread.

Then David said to Ahimelech, "Then have you not here a spear or a sword at hand? For I have brought neither my sword nor my weapons with me, because the king's business required haste." And the priest said, "The sword of Goliath the Philistine, whom you struck down in the Valley of Elah, behold, it is here wrapped in a cloth." (1 Samuel 21:8–9)

So David ran off with his bread and Goliath's enormous sword. The bad news is that one of Saul's servants, Doeg, was there. He heard the whole conversation.

Doeg went back to Saul and told him what he had heard. Saul summoned all the priests of Nob to stand before him and said,

"Why have you conspired against me, you and the son of Jesse?" (1 Samuel 22:13). He thought they were hiding David from him.

Ahimelech was shocked! He thought he had helped David fulfill a secret mission for Saul. But Saul didn't believe him, and in his anger, Saul commanded that every man, woman, child, and animal in Nob be killed.

Only one man escaped to tell David, and when David heard, he was upset. He had not killed them himself, but he had started a domino effect. David could have made other choices. He could have asked a farmer for some food, or he could have told Ahimelech the truth and let Ahimelech decide whether or not to help him. But his fearful lies caused the deaths of everyone in the village.

Think of a situation (imaginary or real) where you're afraid and are tempted to lie. What might happen if you lie? How could the domino effect cause someone else to get hurt? Ask God to help you trust him, even when you're afraid.

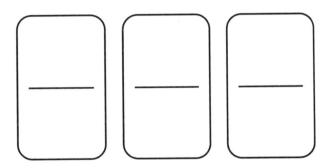

Mother's Prayer Section

Ask each other: Have you ever faked being
sick to get out of something?

After David left Nob, he made a strange choice: he ran to Gath for safety. What was Gath? It was a city filled with his enemies, the Philistines!

When he showed up, they whispered among themselves:

"Isn't this the guy that killed Goliath? He's even carrying Goliath's sword!"

"Hey, this is the dude that killed 200 of us as a wedding present!"

Unsurprisingly, they didn't trust him, and they arrested him instead.

Once David discovered that Gath wasn't a safe place, he brushed up on his acting skills by pretending to be insane! He even let spit run down his beard. Now that's attention to detail. As you can probably guess, it's rather gross to see someone with spit all over their beard. Disgusted, the king of Gath sent him away instead of killing him.

David was so grateful to be alive that he wrote one of his most famous prayer songs. Let's look at a few things he prayed:

I sought the Lord, and he answered me
and delivered me from all my fears.
Those who look to him are radiant,
and their faces shall never be ashamed.
(Psalm 34:4–5)

David said his face was radiant, not because he had wiped the spit out of his beard, but because he looked to God. I think he knew he made a mistake going to Gath for safety instead of trusting God. He had to remind himself who actually protected him.

Here's a verse that's kind of funny when you know why David wrote this song:

Keep your tongue from evil
and your lips from speaking deceit.
(Psalm 34:13)

Deceit is when you trick someone, which is exactly what he did to get out of Gath without being killed! Sometimes we have to remind ourselves about God's truth, like David did here.

There's one more part of this psalm that I want to show you:

The eyes of the Lord are toward the righteous
and his ears toward their cry.

....

When the righteous cry for help, the Lord hears
and delivers them out of all their troubles.
The Lord is near to the brokenhearted
and saves the crushed in spirit.
(Psalm 34:15, 17–18)

David tried trusting in humans to protect him. Instead, he discovered that he could trust God because

- God sees,
- God hears,
- God delivers,
- God is near, and
- God saves.

Write out one of the verses or passages in this chapter in the space below, as your own prayer to God.

....

....

....

....

Mother's Prayer Section

....

....

....

....

....

....

....

....

....

19 TRUSTING GOD AGAIN
Psalm 56

Ask each other: What's the biggest trouble you ever got into?

The psalm we're going to read today also comes from the time that David was in Gath. The title says it was written "when the Philistines seized him in Gath," so he probably wrote this from a jail cell.

Imagine how it would feel to be arrested. What would you say to God? I might pray, "God help me get out of here!" Let's see what we can learn from David's prayer.

First, he told God what had happened:

Be gracious to me, O God, for man tramples on me;
all day long an attacker oppresses me;
my enemies trample on me all day long,
for many attack me proudly.
(Psalm 56:1–2)

Then David wrote one of the most famous phrases in the Psalms:

When I am afraid,
I put my trust in you.
(Psalm 56:3)

What do you put your trust in when you're afraid? Do you put your trust in the police? Good locks on your doors? A light in the hallway? The best place to put our trust is always in God. David tells us why in the next section:

In God, whose word I praise,
in God I trust; I shall not be afraid.
What can flesh do to me?
(Psalm 56:4)

David knew that humans (flesh) couldn't harm his soul. The worst that humans could do to him was kill his body. Jesus said something similar in Matthew 10:28: "Do not fear those who kill the body but cannot kill the soul." David and Jesus knew that God is so much bigger and more powerful than anything that could hurt your body. Because you are part of Jesus's family, your soul is safe forever.

David also knew that God cared deeply for him. He said,

> You have kept count of my tossings;
> put my tears in your bottle.
> Are they not in your book?
> (Psalm 56:8)

God knows when you toss and turn all night. He knows every tear you cry, and even if he doesn't take away the sadness or worries, he's with you through all of it.

God wants nothing more than for you to be with him. Jesus called this "abundant life." When you pray, remember that God wants to help you "walk before God in the light of life" (Psalm 56:13), so don't be afraid to ask him for help!

Draw a bottle. Inside, write the things that make you afraid or sad. Then put your hand on the page and say, "When I am afraid, I put my trust in you, God, because you love me."

Mother's Prayer Section

20 COMPLAINING THROUGH PRAYER
1 Samuel 22:1–2 and Psalm 142

Ask each other: What's something you complain about a lot?

Complaining. We all do it. Babies complain about having a poopy diaper, parents complain about changing diapers, big siblings complain about having to smell diapers, and grandparents complain about all the complaining! It's one of our big human problems.

It's good to be cheerful, but sometimes things really are bad and it's not healthy to pretend everything is fine. David had to run away from Israel because Saul kept trying to kill him. He tried to find safety in Gath, but that turned out bad too. So where could he go? It seemed like everyone wanted him dead, so he hid in a cave.

While he was there, he wrote another prayer: Psalm 142. Let's read part of it, because it teaches us another way to pray.

With my voice I cry out to the Lord;
with my voice I plead for mercy to the Lord.
I pour out my complaint before him;
I tell my trouble before him.

....

Look to the right and see:
there is none who takes notice of me;
no refuge remains to me;
no one cares for my soul.
(Psalm 142:1–2, 4)

David the God-chaser complained to God! Doesn't that seem strange? But it's actually very healthy. Instead of telling everyone around him about his problems, he told God. Usually we do the opposite: we tell only other people what's wrong, and we forget to tell God. But God wants to hear it! He's not afraid of our problems.

But let's read on and see *how* we can talk to God about our problems in a healthy way. After his complaint, David wrote this:

Attend to my cry,
for I am brought very low!
Deliver me from my persecutors,
for they are too strong for me!
(Psalm 142:6)

David didn't just complain. He asked God for help. He told God to listen to him and save him. Finally, he wrote that he knew God would help him. He knew he wouldn't be alone forever:

The righteous will surround me,
for you will deal bountifully with me.
(Psalm 142:7)

And God did help David. While he was hiding, David's brothers and friends came to join him, and soon there were 400 men in that cave. David was no longer alone. Yet again, God showed David that he was faithful when David faithfully trusted him.

Tell God about a problem in your life (either draw it or write it). Ask him to help you with this problem!

Mother's Prayer Section

....

....

....

....

....

....

Say to each other: Tell me about a time when
you needed someone else's help.

When you don't know how to finish your schoolwork, what do you do? Do you keep staring at it, hoping it will suddenly make sense? Do you ask your mom for help?

Let's see what David did when he needed help!

While he was hiding from Saul, David heard that Philistines were attacking an Israelite city called Keilah. It seems like Saul was too busy chasing David to protect his people. So "David inquired of the Lord, 'Shall I go and attack these Philistines?' And the Lord said to David, 'Go and attack the Philistines and save Keilah'" (1 Samuel 23:2).

David's men thought it was a terrible idea! So David double-checked with God and was told, "Go down to Keilah, for I will give the Philistines into your hand" (1 Samuel 23:4).

David led his men to Keilah, just as God told him to, and just as God promised, they beat the Philistines and saved the town. Hurrah! Except Saul heard about it and thought to himself, "God has given him into my hand, for he has shut himself in by entering a town that has gates and bars" (1 Samuel 23:7). He ordered his army to march on Keilah.

Sometimes, even though we obey God, things don't turn out how we expected. Maybe you chose to show kindness to a mean kid on the playground, only for him to pick on you even more! Or maybe you chose to give most of your savings to a homeless shelter, and then you didn't have enough money to get a Slurpee with your friend.

In David's story, he could have whined, "But, God, *you* said to go help these people! And now Saul's going to get me!" Instead of whining, he asked God to guide him again. God helped David and his men escape Saul's trap.

The Bible says that "Saul sought him every day, but God did not give him into his hand" (1 Samuel 23:14). Both men might have felt like God had given David into Saul's hands, but because David kept asking God for help and guidance, he was saved.

Following God isn't always easy, but it is always worth it.

What is something you're dealing with right now? Ask God what he wants you to do. Then practice listening! God might speak to you through the words of the Bible, but he will also give you ideas that you couldn't have thought of by yourself.

....

....

....

....

Mother's Prayer Section

....

....

....

....

....

Say to each other: Tell me about
something you are waiting for.

Saul chased David all over Israel, trying to kill him. Everywhere David went, Saul hunted him in a deadly game of hide-and-seek.

One day, David and his men heard Saul's group coming. They snuck into a cave, tiptoeing into the darkness in the back. They quietly hoped Saul's men would pass by. Instead, something else happened. Saul went into the cave to go to the bathroom. By himself.

> *The men of David said to him, "Here is the day of which the Lord said to you, 'Behold, I will give your enemy into your hand, and you shall do to him as it shall seem good to you.'"* (1 Samuel 24:4)

It seemed perfect. In fact, it seemed like God had made this happen. No more waiting; it was David's turn to be king! But David chose not to kill Saul. Instead, he cut off a corner of Saul's robe.

That seems like a weird move, right? Robes don't seem like a big deal to us, but here's why it matters. Years earlier, Saul had torn a piece of Samuel's robe in his desperation to get Samuel (and God) to stay with him. Samuel told him that the torn robe was a picture of God tearing the kingdom from Saul.

Saul's robe was also important: in ancient cultures, a king's robe reminded people that he was the rightful leader. When Jonathan and David pledged friendship, Jonathan took off his robe and gave it to David. It was a sign that God had chosen David as the next king.

So in the darkness of that cave, David cut off a corner of Saul's robe, showing that he didn't think Saul was the rightful king anymore. He got impatient and wanted his turn to be king.

Afterward, he felt really guilty. He remembered that God would decide when Saul's turn was over. So he apologized and promised never to kill Saul. David chose again to trust God and to be patient for his turn to be king.

Saul understood what David had done by cutting the robe, and he said, "I know that you shall surely be king, and that the kingdom of Israel shall be established in your hand" (1 Samuel 24:20). It was only a matter of time now, and they both knew it.

It's hard to be patient, isn't it? What are you waiting for? Draw a picture of it, and ask God to help you wait patiently.

Mother's Prayer Section

....

....

....

....

....

Ask each other: Who is the smartest person you know?

Have you ever been about to do something really dumb when someone stopped you? Like maybe you were going to jump from the highest slide at the park, but your mom yelled, "*Nooooooo!*" Or maybe you were about to light something on fire, and a friend said, "That's a bad idea." (Please say you listened!)

In today's verses, David was about to make a really bad choice. His men had protected the shepherds of a man named Nabal. When sheep-shearing time came, David's men asked Nabal for some food. Nabal just sneered at them and sent them back to David.

When they finished telling their story, David commanded all his men to strap on their swords. He wanted revenge. David planned to kill every single male that belonged to Nabal's household. His family, his servants, and his shepherds would all die.

Nabal's wife, Abigail, got wind of Nabal's rudeness, and she immediately loaded up many donkeys with food and led them through the mountains. When she found David and his men, she bowed before him. Abigail reminded David that God would deal with his enemies and asked him to ignore Nabal, whose name meant "fool."

David replied:

Blessed be your discretion, and blessed be you, who have kept me this day from bloodguilt and from working salvation with my own hand! For as surely as the Lord, the God of Israel, lives, who has restrained me from hurting you, unless you had hurried and come to meet me, truly by morning there had not been left to Nabal so much as one male. (1 Samuel 25:33–34)

Even David needed to be reminded to make good choices. And you know what? God did deal with David's enemy. That battle was the Lord's, just as much as the battle with Goliath had been.

Abigail left the food for David and his men and went home. "In the morning, when the wine had gone out of Nabal, his wife told him these things, and his heart died within him, and he became as a stone. And about ten days later the Lord struck Nabal, and he died" (1 Samuel 25:37–38).

When David discovered this, he praised God for keeping him from doing wrong. Then he married Abigail so he could keep her wisdom around! Smart guy.

Ask God to help you think of some wise people who can help when you have a tough choice to make. As you think of names, write them down.

....

....

....

....

Mother's Prayer Section

....

....

....

....

Ask each other: Have you ever had a friend try to get you to do something you weren't supposed to?

Sometimes friends can be amazing, like Jonathan. When David was hiding from Saul, Jonathan came to him and reminded him to trust in God. What a great friend! David had another friend too, but he wasn't such a great example.

Saul was chasing David (again), and this time he brought 3,000 men with him. They tried to find David, but he found them first. Imagine David and a few friends lying on their stomachs in the bushes, watching Saul and his men set up camp for the night.

David looked at his friends and asked, "Who will go down with me into the camp to Saul?" (1 Samuel 26:6). Abishai volunteered. Under cover of darkness, they snuck into camp, managing to get right up to Saul.

> And there lay Saul sleeping within the encampment, with his spear stuck in the ground at his head, and Abner and the army lay around him. Then Abishai said to David, "God has given your enemy into your hand this day. Now please let me pin him to the earth with one stroke of the spear." (1 Samuel 26:7–8)

David had his chance to get rid of Saul once and for all. Abishai had volunteered to kill Saul for him, so he didn't have to do it himself. If they snuck out quietly, no one would ever know they had been there!

But David knew that if Abishai did this, it would actually be David's fault for letting him do it. So he told Abishai, "Do not destroy him, for who can put out his hand against the Lord's anointed and be guiltless?" (1 Samuel 26:9).

David chose again to trust that God had a plan to make him king. (Sometimes we all have to remind ourselves that God is still in charge!) Instead of killing Saul, they grabbed his spear and water jug and snuck back out of the camp.

This time there were no apologies. David stood on a far hill and held up the spear and jug, proving to Saul that he could have killed him but didn't. David knew he had done the right thing and that God would reward him.

Copy this verse (either on your own or together with your mom) as a reminder of what David learned:

The Lord rewards every man for his righteousness and his faithfulness. (1 Samuel 26:23)

....

....

....

....

Mother's Prayer Section

....

....

....

....

Say to each other: Tell me about a time you were scared.

After chasing David for years, Saul finally said, "I have sinned. Return, my son David, for I will no more do you harm, because my life was precious in your eyes this day. Behold, I have acted foolishly, and have made a great mistake" (1 Samuel 26:21).

But Saul had chased after him for so long that David didn't really believe him. "Then David said in his heart, 'Now I shall perish one day by the hand of Saul. There is nothing better for me than that I should escape to the land of the Philistines'" (1 Samuel 27:1).

Say what now?

David had trusted God so much that he chose not to kill Saul when he had the chance. Twice. And now, for some reason, David gave up hope that God would keep his promises! He assumed that Saul would kill him.

In his fear, he decided to escape to the Philistines (again). Achish, the prince of Gath, loved him and even gave him an entire village, named Ziklag. While they lived with the Philistines, David and his men did some pretty awful things.

> *David and his men went up and made raids against the Geshurites, the Girzites, and the Amalekites....[They] would leave neither man nor woman alive, but would take away the sheep, the oxen, the donkeys, the camels, and the garments, and come back to Achish. (1 Samuel 27:8–9)*

When Achish asked where the plunder was from, David lied and said it came from Israelite towns. In order for his trick to work, David had to kill every person in those towns so they wouldn't escape and tattle to the Philistines. Achish thought David was so great that he made him his bodyguard for life, because he assumed that David hated the Israelites and that they hated him back.

Out of fear, David pretended to be besties with a Philistine prince and killed a lot of people. Isn't it wild how fear can make us forget God's promises? Let's remember this promise from God:

Have I not commanded you? Be strong and courageous. Do not be frightened, and do not be dismayed, for the Lord your God is with you wherever you go. (Joshua 1:9)

We don't need to be afraid. Why? Because God is with us.

Write down or say Joshua 1:9 out loud. Remind yourself of it when you start to become afraid! You could even create a poster to hang in your room.

Mother's Prayer Section

Ask each other: Have you ever pretended to be
fine when you were actually really upset?

Have you ever heard any of these sentences?

"Big boys don't cry."

"Buck up."

"Stop being a wimp."

Those phrases are often said by people who think that it's not manly to show emotions. But it's not true. Being sad, feeling afraid, or crying aren't signs of weakness. Even Jesus cried! Recent scientific studies have shown that if we always pretend to be strong, or pretend like everything is OK, we can actually make ourselves sick.

Once when David and his men came back from a trip, they discovered that their village, Ziklag, had been burned to the ground and their families kidnapped by Amalekites.

Then David and the people who were with him raised their voices and wept until they had no more strength to weep. (1 Samuel 30:4)

David's men were not only sad but also angry. Since the Amalekites were gone, they got angry at David instead.

David was greatly distressed, for the people spoke of stoning him, because all the people were bitter in soul, each for his sons and daughters. (1 Samuel 30:6)

David could have run away. He could have pretended to know exactly what to do. Instead, the Bible says, "David strengthened himself in the Lord his God" (1 Samuel 30:6).

The truth is, we don't need to pretend to be strong, because God is strong for us. David wrote in Psalm 18:2:

The Lord is my rock and my fortress and my deliverer,
my God, my rock, in whom I take refuge,
my shield, and the horn of my salvation, my stronghold.

We don't know exactly how David found strength in God. Maybe he took a walk and prayed. Maybe he reminded himself how God had cared for him before. Afterward, he and the priest asked God what to do next. God showed them what to do.

David led his 600 men to chase after the Amalekites. Their enemies were partying in the countryside, proud of all they had stolen. David and his men fought them and won, and every single person from their village was rescued.

David looked to God for strength and found more strength and wisdom than he would have found inside himself. You can do that too.

Draw a graph showing how much strength and wisdom you think you have inside you, apart from God. Then ask God to give you more! He loves when we ask for his strength and his wisdom.

Mother's Prayer Section

Say to each other: Tell me about a time
when something felt really unfair.

Have you ever heard the saying "Life isn't fair"? Maybe you studied hard for a test and failed, but you know another kid who cheated and did well. Or maybe your little sister always gets to choose the first Popsicle and takes your favorite flavor.

But unfairness isn't always bad. Let's take a peek at what happened when David and his men returned from fighting the Amalekites. Not only had they gotten their families back, but they also took plunder from the Amalekites. (This was how soldiers got paid—when they won a battle, they'd take their share of the plunder, which was usually animals. No gold or jewels here, unfortunately!) The trouble was, only 400 of David's soldiers had done the fighting, because 200 of them had been too exhausted to even walk to the fight!

> *Then David came to the two hundred men who had been too exhausted to follow David, and who had been left at the brook Besor. And they went out to meet David and to meet the people who were with him. And when David came near to the people he greeted them. Then all the wicked and worthless fellows among the men who had gone with David said, "Because they did not go with us, we will not give them any of the spoil that we have recovered, except that each man may lead away his wife and children, and depart." (1 Samuel 30:21–22)*

That seems fair, don't you think? Every soldier would get his family back, but only the men who risked their lives would get a share of the plunder.

But David didn't want to do what was fair; he wanted to do what was right. This is like a verse from earlier in the Bible:

> Beware lest you say in your heart, "My power and the might of my hand have gotten me this wealth." You shall remember the Lord your God, for it is he who gives you power to get wealth. (Deuteronomy 8:17–18)

David knew that everything they had was from God and that God had given them the victory. So he made a new rule that those who stayed with the supplies would get just as much as those who did the fighting. It might not have been fair, but it was right!

Draw a picture or write about a time something felt unfair. Then thank God for two things that God did give you in that situation.

Mother's Prayer Section

2 Samuel 1:1–12

Say to each other: Tell me about a close call
(a time when something bad seemed to be
about to happen, but then it didn't).

Remember when David and his men returned to Ziklag to find their families stolen by Amalekites? That entire journey and battle is part of a bigger story, so we're going to zoom out and look at the bigger picture for a moment.

Because Saul kept trying to kill him, David ran to the Philistines for safety (again). Achish, the prince of Gath, liked him. While David was there, he tricked Achish to make him think he was loyal to the Philistines, so the next time the Philistines went to war with Israel, Achish wanted to bring his new best friend along. The rest of the Philistines weren't so keen because they remembered that David was famous for killing Philistines. They thought he might betray them. So David and his men went home to Ziklag, and you know what happened there.

While David and his men were fighting Amalekites and dividing plunder, the Philistines and Israelites battled. The Israelites lost, and Saul and Jonathan both died.

When a messenger came to tell David the news, he expected David to be happy because Saul had been his enemy. Instead, "David took hold of his clothes and tore them, and so did all the men who were with him. And they mourned and wept and fasted until evening for Saul and for Jonathan his son and for the people of the Lord and for the house of Israel, because they had fallen by the sword" (2 Samuel 1:11–12).

The king of Israel was dead, and David could finally take his place as God's chosen king.

What do you think would have happened if David had gone with the Philistines and been part of the army that killed Saul? Do you think the Israelites would have wanted him as their king?

David had become attached to the Philistines, but God knew that he couldn't be part of the battle that killed Saul. So he caused the other Philistine commanders to be suspicious of him and send him away. It was good timing because he was able to rescue his family, but also because it meant that no one could blame him for Saul's death.

David chased God instead of chasing the kingship, and God did the rest. You can trust God to guide and protect you too.

What does it look like for God to protect you? Write a prayer for God to protect you, or draw a picture of God protecting you.

Mother's Prayer Section

29 PATIENCE (AGAIN)
2 Samuel 2:1–7

Say to each other: Tell me about a time when you
had to wait a long while for something special.

Most people aren't very good at waiting. We don't want to grind grain and bake a loaf of bread; we want to buy it in a bag from the store so we can eat it right away. We don't want to wait until we've saved enough money for something big; we want to borrow money so we can get it now.

At the beginning of this book, we read that David was chosen by God as the future king over all of Israel. We are more than halfway through this prayer journal and he's still not king! That's a crazy amount of waiting. But through it all, David has been (mostly) patient. He refused to force it to happen by killing Saul. He waited until God decided that it was time for him to be king. While he was waiting, he grew closer to God, wrote some amazing psalms, and became a stronger leader. Finally, when David was 30 years old, it finally happened:

After this David inquired of the Lord, "Shall I go up into any of the cities of Judah?" And the Lord said to him, "Go up." David said, "To which shall I go up?" And he said, "To Hebron." So David went up there, and his two wives also, Ahinoam of Jezreel and Abigail the widow of Nabal of Carmel. And David brought up his men who were with him, everyone with his household, and they lived in the towns of Hebron. And the men of Judah came, and there they anointed David king over the house of Judah. (2 Samuel 2:1–4)

Hold on, did you catch that last bit? Who anointed David king? That's right, the men of Judah. Israel was divided into 12 tribes, each named after one of Jacob's 12 sons. So David was king, but only over the tribe of Judah! Saul's son Ish-Bosheth was still king over the rest of Israel.

I don't know about you, but I feel frustrated for David. After waiting for over 10 years, he got to be king of only one part of Israel! I wonder if he questioned whether God was ever going to keep his promise.

It took another seven and a half years of war with Ish-Bosheth, but David did finally become king of all Israel.

What are you waiting for right now? Draw a comic of you waiting. Use a speech bubble to say something to God.

Mother's Prayer Section

....

....

....

....

Ask each other: Have you ever known
someone who felt like an enemy?

Humans have always known exactly what to do with an enemy: kill him. Cain killed his brother Abel. Pharaoh killed Israelites. Samson killed Philistines. David killed Goliath. When someone was an enemy, you got rid of them. Most of the world still works like that. Although in most countries we don't personally kill our enemies anymore, we might still try to get revenge.

Jesus came to show us a different way. Jesus said, "You have heard that it was said, 'You shall love your neighbor and hate your enemy.' But I say to you, love your enemies and pray for those who persecute you" (Matthew 5:43–44).

Jesus lived a life of radical love toward everyone, including his enemies. Even when he was dying on the cross he said, "Father, forgive them, for they know not what they do" (Luke 23:34).

This is a hard way to live, isn't it? But remember, the Bible tells us about David, a man who had the Holy Spirit on him, helping him to be a God-chaser. David wasn't perfect, but he does show that it's possible to love your enemies (at least, some of them).

Remember how David treated Saul? Even though Saul repeatedly tried to kill him, David refused to hurt him back. When Saul finally died, an Amalekite ran to tell David the news. He thought David would reward him. Instead, David wrote a song for Saul. (He also killed the Amalekite—he certainly wasn't perfect!)

David lived out this proverb: "Do not rejoice when your enemy falls, and let not your heart be glad when he stumbles" (Proverbs 24:17).

The same thing happened when Ish-Bosheth, Saul's son, was king over Israel and David was king over Judah. David's army and Ish-Bosheth's army fought over Israel for seven years. Finally, two men killed Ish-Bosheth and took his head to David (ew!). They thought he'd be impressed and that he'd reward them for killing his enemy. They were wrong.

David knew that God would deal with his enemies, so he didn't need to take revenge. Jesus took this idea even further. He didn't just say, "Don't hurt your enemies," but commanded that we actually love and pray for our enemies.

This is not easy, but David's life shows us that it is possible when the Holy Spirit helps us.

Write the name of someone who feels like an enemy to you or your family. Now pray for that person.

....

....

Mother's Prayer Section

....

....

....

....

....

....

....

Ask each other: What kind of person
would make a terrible king?

When David was finally chosen as the king over all of Israel, the leaders reminded him of something: "And the Lord said to you, 'You shall be shepherd of my people Israel'" (2 Samuel 5:2).

We might think that they called him a shepherd because he used to take care of sheep, but back then rulers were sometimes likened to shepherds. And this title wasn't just an Israelite thing. We have old writings that show us that Assyrians, Egyptians, and Babylonians sometimes thought of their rulers as shepherds too. Being a shepherd of people was a noble and royal task, given by God. Even though we think of actual shepherds as being rather dirty and smelly from living outside with animals, people in these ancient cultures considered it an honor to be a Shepherd King.

How is a good king like a shepherd?

A shepherd is responsible for finding food and water for his sheep, protecting them from enemies, and rescuing them when they wander away. Like a shepherd, a good king should take care of his people, protect them, and rescue them.

A Shepherd King wouldn't boss people around just for the fun of it but would sacrifice himself for the good of his people. He would be a servant, not a slave master.

David's people called him the shepherd of Israel, but there's another, perfect Shepherd King. Do you know who it is?

It's the guy who said this:

I am the good shepherd. The good shepherd lays down his life for the sheep. He who is a hired hand and not a shepherd, who does not own the sheep, sees the wolf coming and leaves the sheep and flees, and the wolf snatches them and scatters them. He flees because he is a hired hand and cares nothing for the sheep. I am the good shepherd. I know my own and my own know me, just as the Father knows me and I know the Father; and I lay down my life for the sheep. (John 10:11–15)

You know who said this, right? Jesus. He is the ultimate Shepherd King. David did his best to care for God's people, but they weren't technically his people. They were God's people. He was more like a hired hand, chosen by God to care for his people.

In John 10:27, Jesus said, "My sheep hear my voice, and I know them, and they follow me." What does God's voice sound like to you? How do you know when you've heard from him? Write down your answers, and ask Jesus to help you listen to him.

....

....

....

....

Mother's Prayer Section

....

....

....

....

Say to each other: Tell me about a time
you disobeyed and got in trouble.

Have you ever taken a vacation to the sun? What a crazy question, right? You wouldn't even dream of getting that close to the sun because it would kill you. The sun is set apart because of its awesomeness.

That's like God. God is loving and kind but also perfect and holy, and he is set apart because of that. When Moses went close to the burning bush, God said, "Do not come near; take your sandals off your feet, for the place on which you are standing is holy ground" (Exodus 3:5).

The Israelites built a special box called the Ark of the Covenant, which represented God's holy presence on earth. Just like the sun, no one could touch it. It was holy. God gave very strict rules around how to carry it. If you've ever seen a movie where a king or queen was carried on a litter, this is exactly how the Ark was to be carried. There were poles on either side, and only the family of Kohath was allowed to lift the Ark on its poles.

Many years before David lived, the Philistines had stolen the Ark. They treated it like a good luck charm, and God punished them severely. They put the Ark on a new cart and sent it back to Israel. When David became king, he wanted to bring the Ark to Jerusalem. The Israelites set it on a new cart and danced for joy as cows pulled the Ark toward Jerusalem.

Wait, did you catch that? Did David move the Ark like God had commanded, or like the Philistines did?

When Saul was king, he also chose to do things his own way. Samuel told him, "To obey is better than sacrifice, and to listen than the fat of rams" (1 Samuel 15:22). God wants obedience, not gifts.

David's disobedience had a high price. A cow stumbled, the cart tipped, and Uzzah reached out to steady it. And then he died because no one, *no one* was supposed to touch the Ark. David was angry with God but also with himself. He had caused this by not moving the Ark the right way. It was like taking a trip to the sun and expecting no one to get hurt.

Have you ever disobeyed someone like a parent, coach, or teacher and regretted it later? Disobedience can hurt a lot of people. Tell God about a time you disobeyed, and write, "I'm sorry."

....

....

....

....

Mother's Prayer Section

....

....

....

....

....

....

Say to each other: Tell me about the most amazing thing that's ever happened to you.

How do you celebrate when something great happens? Do you scream and jump? Smile and nod? Throw a party?

Everyone celebrates differently, even David!

Remember when David first tried to bring home the Ark, but he didn't follow God's directions? Three months later David was ready to try again. This time, he did it God's way:

> And when those who bore the ark of the Lord had gone six steps, he sacrificed an ox and a fattened animal. And David danced before the Lord with all his might. And David was wearing a linen ephod. So David and all the house of Israel brought up the ark of the Lord with shouting and with the sound of the horn. (2 Samuel 6:13–15)

Imagine the noise of shouting, horns, harps, and cymbals. Imagine the smell of sweat and animals and the tang of blood. Imagine the feel of the hot sun on your face and the jostling of people trying to see the Ark pass by. It was a parade, a church service, and a carnival all rolled into one.

As the Ark reached Jerusalem, David "blessed the people in the name of the Lord of hosts and distributed among all the people, the whole multitude of Israel, both men and women, a cake of bread, a portion of meat, and a cake of raisins to each one" (2 Samuel 6:18–19).

David leaped and danced before God, prayed for his people, offered sacrifices, and gave gifts.

Remember Michal, his first wife? When he came home, she was angry and annoyed with him.

But David wasn't ashamed of his excitement. He said,

It was before the Lord, who chose me above your father and above all his house, to appoint me as prince over Israel, the people of the Lord—and I will celebrate before the Lord. I will make myself yet more contemptible than this, and I will be abased in your eyes. (2 Samuel 6:21–22)

Those big words mean this: "God gave me all this and I will celebrate him how I want, even if I look silly."

Not everyone has to celebrate God through dancing and music and parties, but sometimes it can feel amazing to just hoot and holler for God. Try it right now!

Draw a picture of yourself. Use a speech bubble to write a prayer of praise to God.

Mother's Prayer Section

34 RUN THE RACE
1 Chronicles 16:8–36

Ask each other: Have you ever been in a race?

Sometimes we run races with just one friend. But most times, we run races when other people are watching.

A really long race is called a marathon. A marathon can be painful and tiring, but one of the best parts of any race is all the people gathered along the road, cheering the runners on. They shout and clap and give high fives to the people running past, encouraging runners to keep going, even when they're exhausted and just want to quit.

Our Christian life is like that! You and I are like runners in a marathon, except that our race is our whole life. It can be hard to chase God sometimes, but Hebrews 12:1–2 says, "Since we are surrounded by so great a cloud of witnesses, let us also lay aside every weight, and sin which clings so closely, and let us run with endurance the race that is set before us, looking to Jesus, the founder and perfecter of our faith."

The "cloud of witnesses" are God's faithful people who have lived before us, and they cheer us on from heaven as we run after Jesus.

What does this have to do with David? I'm glad you asked! After he brought the Ark to Jerusalem, he wrote a song in which he reminded the Israelites about all that God had done for the people that went before them.

Remember his covenant forever,
the word that he commanded, for a thousand generations,
the covenant that he made with Abraham,
his sworn promise to Isaac,
which he confirmed to Jacob as a statute,
to Israel as an everlasting covenant.
(1 Chronicles 16:15–18)

David reminded his people that God had been faithful to Abraham, Isaac, Jacob, and all of Israel. These people could cheer on the Israelites, just like the Christians who lived before you are cheering you on! In fact, I bet Abraham, Isaac, and Jacob even cheer for you.

There are so many people who are cheering for you as you chase after God. Even those who aren't alive anymore are cheering you on from heaven! So let's run that race of life together.

List as many Christians as you can think of. Write them all down (if you have enough space). All those people are cheering you on, either from earth or from heaven. Thank God for them!

....

....

....

....

Mother's Prayer Section

....

....

....

....

Ask each other: What is the best gift anyone ever gave you?

Gifts are one amazing way to say thank you to someone. But what kind of gift do you get someone who gave you a whole kingdom? A medal? A crown? Your firstborn son? As tricky as that sounds, now imagine choosing a gift for someone who owns the whole universe.

That's the position David was in. God kept his promise to give him a kingdom. He helped David beat all his enemies, including the enemies inside him, such as impatience, revenge, and pride. So David wanted to give God a gift. He knew that the Ark of the Covenant was still in a tent while he, the king, lived in a palace. David wanted to build a house for God (also called a temple).

God basically said to David, "Thanks, but no thanks. I'm good." Instead of accepting his thank-you gift, God told David that he was going to give him even more.

God told David,

When your days are fulfilled and you lie down with your fathers, I will raise up your offspring after you, who shall come from your body, and I will establish his kingdom. He shall build a house for my name, and I will establish the throne of his kingdom forever. (2 Samuel 7:12–13)

David probably thought God was talking about David's son, who would build a temple for God. But we know that Solomon's kingdom didn't last forever, and although he did build a temple, it didn't last forever either.

God wasn't talking about Solomon. He said, "And your house and your kingdom shall be made sure forever before me. Your throne shall be established forever" (2 Samuel 7:16).

David wanted to build a house for God, but God wanted to build a house for David. His own kind of house though, not one built with bricks. Instead, God would build a house and kingdom out of the lives of those who love and follow David's great-great (and many more greats) grandson: Jesus.

God didn't give this incredible promise and gift just for David. It was for you and me too. God doesn't need us to build a house for him. He wants us to be part of his house, his family. And we can, because of Jesus.

Make a list of all the things that God has done for you or given you. Try to go beyond "my family and house," and think about the spiritual gifts God has given you too.

....

....

....

....

Mother's Prayer Section

....

....

....

....

2 Samuel 8:15

Ask each other: How would you describe
a kid who is a good leader?

It's easy to spot a bad leader. They're the person who takes the good things for themselves, takes credit for other people's work, and lays the blame for their own mistakes on others. No one likes living with a bad leader.

The Bible says that after becoming king, "David reigned over all Israel. And David administered justice and equity to all his people" (2 Samuel 8:15). In other Bible translations, this verse says that David did "what was just and right for all his people" (New International Version).

That sounds great, doesn't it? But what exactly does that mean?

We could say that doing what is *right* means helping other people, being kind and good to each person you meet.

Doing what is *just*, or administering *justice*, means making things right for a lot of people. There are many things in this world that are wrong because leaders have made bad choices. Doing justice means fixing big problems so that many people can live better lives.

Imagine yourself playing with a group of kids at the park. There are two kids who can't play the game because they can't reach the monkey bars. How could you do what is just and right?

If you're doing what is *right*, you would help those kids. Maybe you could lift up a smaller child so they can reach the monkey bars, or change a rule so they don't need the monkey bars.

If you're doing what is *just*, you would choose to solve the problem for many kids. You could encourage the other kids to change the game so that little kids can join in. Or, if the kids can't reach because they are disabled, you could ask your town to put in better playgrounds!

Doing what is just and right can be hard, and that's one reason Jesus came to live with us. Check out this promise from God:

> Behold, the days are coming, declares the Lord, when I will fulfill the promise I made to the house of Israel and the house of Judah. In those days and at that time I will cause a righteous Branch to spring up for David, and he shall execute justice and righteousness in the land. (Jeremiah 33:14–15)

Jesus is the ultimate leader, and through his Holy Spirit, he can give you power to be a just and right leader too.

Draw or write what you would do in the playground situation. Make sure to ask God for help!

Mother's Prayer Section

37 KINDNESS IN ACTION

2 Samuel 9:1–13

Ask each other: Have you ever showed kindness
to someone who didn't deserve it?

Let's see what David was up to after being king of Israel for several years. He was Israel's Shepherd King. He did what was just and right for his people, protected them from enemies, and helped them live in safety. Life was good.

David finally turned his attention to Jonathan's family. When they were young, Jonathan had asked David to make this promise:

> But as long as I live, promise me that you will show me kindness because of the Lord. And even when I die, never stop being kind to my family. (1 Samuel 20:14–15)

David intended to keep that promise, even though Jonathan was dead. On the day Saul and Jonathan were killed by Philistines, Jonathan's son Mephibosheth (we'll call him Mephi!) was five years old. His nurse picked him up to run away, but she accidentally dropped him and broke his legs, which crippled him.

By now, Mephi was an adult and had a son of his own. David found them and brought the family to his palace to live! Mephi even ate at the banquet table with David. Mephi was shocked and amazed by David's kindness. Technically, as the grandson of the previous king, Mephi was David's enemy. But David chose kindness instead of revenge.

This is a beautiful picture of what God does for us. You and I are probably not crippled in both legs, but just like Mephi was crippled in his body, we are crippled in our souls. We are sinful, which makes us God's enemies. Just like Mephi, we don't deserve God's kindness. But he gives it anyway.

"In love he predestined us for adoption to himself as sons through Jesus Christ" (Ephesians 1:4–5). Because of God the father's love for his son, we have been brought into God's family.

See what kind of love the Father has given to us, that we should be called children of God. (1 John 3:1)

If you're a Christian, you're part of God's family. He invites you to live with him now and forever. You might not feel like you're sitting at God's banquet table, but that's because it's not a table you can see. God's table is filled with grace, mercy, and power to love him and love others.

Song of Solomon 2:4 says, "He brought me to the banqueting house, and his banner over me was love." Imagine what God's banqueting table looks like. Draw or write about it!

Mother's Prayer Section

Say to each other: Tell me about a
time you hurt someone else.

Today we need to talk about a three-letter word that no one likes to hear. Can you guess what it is?

The word is *sin*. Sin is doing things our way instead of God's way. Each time we know what God wants us to do but we do what we want instead, that's sin. Let's imagine you have a brother who's super annoying. You probably know that it's not right to smack him upside the head, right? But one day he bugs you so much that you punch him. That's sin, because you knew what was right but you chose to do what you wanted instead of the right thing.

Sin separates us from God because he is perfect. Remember when we said that approaching God is a bit like approaching the sun, because his holiness will burn us up?

When Jesus died and came back to life, he made a way for us to get back to God. Let's go back to imagining that God is like the sun. First, Jesus puts a heatproof coating on us. Then, he changes us slowly, from the inside out, so that we become fully heatproof. The fancy words are *justification* and *sanctification*, but just remember that we get an immediate heatproof coating and then we get completely changed. Both give us the ability to be with God.

What does this have to do with David? Well, David sinned. Big time. After Saul was gone and his kingdom was mostly safe, David got lazy. He puttered around on the roof of his palace instead of leading his men to battle. While he was there, he spied a beautiful woman taking a bath. Bathsheba was taking a special bath that Jewish women had to do every month.

And David wanted her. The problem was, she was married to one of his top soldiers (Uriah), so he couldn't make her one of his wives. Under cover of darkness, he sent soldiers to bring her to his palace. He made her pregnant and sent her home.

In one day, David had broken at least two of God's Ten Commandments:

You shall not commit adultery. (Exodus 20:14)
You shall not covet your neighbor's wife. (Exodus 20:17)

Just like David, we often chase the things of the world instead of God.

Tell God about a time you chose to do things your way instead of his way and ended up hurting someone.

....

....

....

....

Mother's Prayer Section

....

....

....

....

....

Say to each other: Tell me about a time you lied
about something and got into even more trouble.

In *The Lord of the Rings*, a good wizard named Gandalf has the chance to take the ring of power. He knows that even though he would originally try to use it for good, the power given by the ring would make him rot inside and turn evil.

Sometimes people say, "Power corrupts." It means that when humans get power, we almost always end up turning bad and hurting others.

David chased God when he was young. Even when Saul was pursuing him, even when his country was at war, David usually followed God. But after a few years of peace, David's power corrupted him.

Remember that he took Uriah's wife? When she got pregnant without her husband around, it was obvious that something was wrong. But instead of owning up to what he did, David broke more of God's rules! It's like he packed some sin into a snowball to try to hide it, but it started rolling down a hill and just kept getting bigger and bigger.

David used his power to cover up what he'd done. He wrote to his commander (instead of talking to God) and brought Uriah back from the battlefield. Instead of telling the truth, he tried to send Uriah home to his wife so everyone would think the baby was Uriah's. But Uriah refused to relax at home because he knew his job was to protect the king.

David was stuck. But still, instead of telling Uriah what he had done, he concocted another plan, using his power again. David gave Uriah a sealed letter to take back to his commander. In the letter David told the commander, "Set Uriah in the forefront of the hardest fighting, and then draw back from him, that he may be struck down, and die" (2 Samuel 11:15).

And that's exactly what happened. Uriah died, and Bathsheba became one of David's wives. Problem solved, right? Except "the thing that David had done displeased the Lord" (2 Samuel 11:27).

David had lied to and murdered Uriah. Oh sure, he didn't pull a sword and kill Uriah himself, but he died because David used his power to tell the commander what to do.

Sin is like that snowball. When we lie about it instead of apologizing, it gets bigger, and people get hurt.

Write down something you might try to lie about. Together, talk about how it could snowball into something bigger. (You can even draw a snowball around it!) Then ask God to help you make the courageous choice to apologize instead of hiding your sin.

....

....

....

....

Mother's Prayer Section

....

....

....

....

Ask each other: Have you ever gotten lost?

Imagine that you are hiking down a trail in the forest. You see a sign that says Dead End, but you choose to walk it anyway because you heard about an amazing waterfall down that trail.

As you walk, the trees get bigger and closer together. It gets darker in the forest. The trail becomes narrower, with more logs to jump over and thornbushes scratching your legs. Eventually, you see that this trail won't lead you to that amazing waterfall, so you turn around.

That is what the biblical word *repentance* means. The word *repent* means "to turn around and move away from sin." You can see this in Acts 3:19–20:

> *Repent therefore, and turn back, that your sins may be blotted out, that times of refreshing may come from the presence of the Lord.*

David went down a path that led nowhere good. He took what wasn't his (Bathsheba), then lied and murdered to cover it up. He thought it was all good, but the prophet Nathan knew it wasn't.

God sent Nathan to David with the following story.

There were two men, one rich and the other poor. The rich man had many animals, but the poor man only had one small lamb. He loved that lamb like a child. He fed it from his table and he snuggled it at night. One day, a guest came to the rich man's home. He didn't want to take one of his own flock, so he took the poor man's lamb and turned it into dinner.

When David heard this story, he was angry at the rich man. But Nathan's story was a parable of David's life. David had stolen someone else's only wife, even though he had many wives of his own.

After listening to Nathan, David told him, "I have sinned against the Lord" (2 Samuel 12:13).

David realized he hadn't just sinned against Bathsheba and Uriah. He had also sinned against God. So he stopped walking the path and turned around. He repented.

As a consequence of David's sin, David and Bathsheba's baby died. But later, David and Bathsheba had another son, named Solomon. God gave Solomon a secret name: Jedidiah. It means "loved by the Lord." David messed up real bad. But when he turned from his sin, God forgave him and made David and Bathsheba's son the future king of Israel.

What does repentance look like to you? Draw a picture of yourself repenting from something, and thank God for his forgiveness!

Say to each other: Tell me about a time you got
in trouble for doing something wrong.

Even if we apologize and repent, there are still consequences. For example, if you kicked your friend, you would (hopefully) apologize, but he still might not want to play with you for a while. Or if you biked ahead of your mom and then hid from her, she might not let you out of her sight for a week!

Sometimes an apology isn't enough; that's what David discovered. When Nathan confronted him about his sin, Nathan had this message from God: "Behold, I will raise up evil against you out of your own house" (2 Samuel 12:11). God was promising that there would be consequences for David's sins.

Because of some of David's bad choices, his family basically fell apart. One of his sons, Amnon, hurt his sister just like David had hurt Bathsheba. David didn't discipline him, so David's other son Absalom killed Amnon in revenge! A few years later, Absalom tried to take over David's kingdom.

Let's look more closely at that time in David's life. We skipped ahead a lot, so he was probably about 60 at this point. Absalom gathered an army, including some of David's trusted advisors. Why would David's friends betray him to serve Absalom instead? Well, one of those trusted advisors was Bathsheba's grandpa. He was probably still angry over the way David had treated his granddaughter.

David worried that Absalom would attack Jerusalem to get to him, so to keep Jerusalem safe, David took his household and his palace soldiers out of the city. He thought his time as king might be over. But even though he knew this was the consequence of his sins, he still praised God. He wrote Psalm 3 while running from Absalom. In it he said,

O Lord, how many are my foes!
Many are rising against me;
many are saying of my soul,
"There is no salvation for him in God."
But you, O Lord, are a shield about me,
my glory, and the lifter of my head.
I cried aloud to the Lord,
and he answered me from his holy hill.
(Psalm 3:1–4)

Even when you do wrong, God will never abandon you. Like David, you can trust God to answer you and love you always.

Draw or write about a time when you faced a consequence for doing wrong. Thank God for always hearing you and being with you, even when you're being disciplined.

Mother's Prayer Section

Say to each other: Tell me about something
you love. Why do you love it?

Do you know what an ambassador is? It's a person who is sent to represent their leader. For instance, the United States sends an ambassador to Canada. The American ambassador represents the president while in Canada. The president tells them what to do and say, and the ambassador does their best to do it.

David knew that Israel was supposed to be an ambassador from God to the whole world. When David got very old, he spoke to his son Solomon, who was to be the next king. He said, "And you, Solomon my son, know the God of your father and serve him with a whole heart and with a willing mind, for the Lord searches all hearts and understands every plan and thought" (1 Chronicles 28:9).

God's plan was to show the world how amazing he is through his ambassadors, the Israelites. But this plan worked properly only when the Israelites followed God with their whole hearts, just like David did. When they didn't follow God, they were terrible ambassadors for God and the world couldn't see how amazing God is.

Did you notice that David didn't say, "serve God with part of your heart"? He didn't want Solomon, or Israel, to serve God only when it was easy.

Jesus gave us a similar command. His first (and most important rule) is this: to "love the Lord your God with all your heart and with all your soul and with all your mind" (Matthew 22:37). Loving God first doesn't mean you can't love other things too, like your mom or cat or video games or soccer, but that God wants to be the center of your heart. When he's in the center, he changes you from the inside out so that you can be a good ambassador and show your world how amazing God is.

Being an ambassador for God doesn't mean you have to be a pastor or a missionary or a Sunday school teacher. You can be God's ambassador by loving and serving others anywhere! You can show others how amazing God is while playing on the monkey bars, while kicking a soccer ball, or even while studying for a test.

You won't be a perfect ambassador, but God knows that. Remember, his Spirit is here to help you love and serve God with your whole heart!

Draw a picture of your heart with God in the middle. If you want to serve God with your whole heart, tell him!

Mother's Prayer Section

1 Chronicles 28:20

Ask each other: What kind of work do you actually like to do?

I know the word *work* can sound like a bad thing, but humans were created to work. God gave Adam and Eve work to do in the Garden of Eden. They took care of the garden and the animals. It's only because of sin that work can sometimes be awful.

Just before he died, David talked to his son Solomon about the work God had called him to do.

> Then David said to Solomon his son, "Be strong and courageous and do it. Do not be afraid and do not be dismayed, for the Lord God, even my God, is with you. He will not leave you or forsake you, until all the work for the service of the house of the Lord is finished." (1 Chronicles 28:20)

Solomon's job was to build a temple for God. It was a huge job that would take many years and cost a lot of money.

But God doesn't give jobs only to kings. God actually has special work for you too, right now. We all start with the same basic job description:

> What does the Lord require of you
> but to do justice, and to love kindness,
> and to walk humbly with your God?
> (Micah 6:8)

God wants us to do justice, love kindness, and walk humbly with him in everything we do.

You might get a more specific job description, though. Maybe you'll feel like God wants you to befriend a lonely kid. Maybe you'll need to stand up against a bully or tell someone about Jesus. God might even ask you to do something that takes your whole life, like becoming a pastor or taking care of orphans or starting a business that helps poor people. Whatever it is, it all comes back to doing justice, loving kindness, and walking humbly with God.

But don't worry. God will never give you a job and leave you alone. Philippians 1:6 reminds us that "he who began a good work in you will bring it to completion at the day of Jesus Christ." Just as David promised that God would help Solomon do the work, God promises to be with you and help you do the good work he's asking you to do.

What kind of work do you think God might want you to do? Ask God to guide you, and talk about your ideas with your mom.

....

....

....

....

Mother's Prayer Section

....

....

....

....

1 Chronicles 29:1–9

Ask each other: Have you ever been
the boss of someone else?

Wouldn't it be nice to be the boss of everyone? You could get everyone else to do the jobs you don't like, get them to bring you a nice cold lemonade, and have them do all your homework. Except...that doesn't sound like the kind of leader I want to serve! Would you want to serve a leader who thinks only about themselves?

When David gave Solomon the big job of building the temple for God, he knew that it was going to be very expensive. He could have told all the people in his kingdom to bring all their gold and jewels and money and fancy fabric for the temple, but David wasn't that kind of leader.

He did collect a lot of gold, silver, iron, and wood, but he also did something else: he gave of his own treasures.

David said to the Israelites,

In addition to all that I have provided for the holy house, I have a treasure of my own of gold and silver, and because of my devotion to the house of my God I give it to the house of my God: 3,000 talents of gold, of the gold of Ophir, and 7,000 talents of refined silver. (1 Chronicles 29:3–4)

That's a lot of treasure! First, David gave his own treasures. Then he asked if anyone else wanted to help build the temple by giving their treasure. And they did! The leaders of each home, the leaders of the 12 tribes, the army commanders, and the officers in David's palace all gave what they could as well. They gave gold, silver, bronze, iron, and precious stones.

Then the people rejoiced because they had given willingly, for with a whole heart they had offered freely to the Lord. David the king also rejoiced greatly. (1 Chronicles 29:9)

Because David set an example of giving, his people were inspired to give as well, and it made them feel amazing! This is called servant leadership, and it is the kind of leadership that made people want to follow Jesus too. If you ever have the chance to be a leader in your class, on the playground, or in your family, I hope that you will choose to be a servant leader!

Think about a time when you might lead others. It can be real or imaginary. Ask God what it looks like to be a servant leader in that situation. Then write or draw it!

Mother's Prayer Section

**Point at something in the room and ask,
Where does that come from?**

Where do the vegetables in your kitchen come from? They probably come from the grocery store, and before that they came from a farm. But before that? They grew in the earth. A farmer planted the seeds and watered them, but God is the one who designed seeds to grow into vegetables.

Where do the clothes in your closet come from? They probably come from a store, and before that they came from a factory. Before the factory, the cotton and linen came from a farm. Again, a farmer planted the seeds and watered them, but God made them grow.

How did you buy those vegetables and clothes? Your mom used money, which came from her bank account, which came from a job. Your mom or dad earned that money, but who gave them the ability to do work? It was God.

Sometimes it can be helpful to think about where things come from in order to see that everything we have is actually a gift from God.

David knew this too. When he divided up the plunder at Ziklag, it was because he knew it was all a gift from God. God owns it all and didn't have to give it to anyone. When David gave his gold and silver toward building the temple, he felt good because he knew God owned it all anyway! He was just giving God's gold and silver back to him.

David told God, "Both riches and honor come from you, and you rule over all. In your hand are power and might, and in your hand it is to make great and to give strength to all" (1 Chronicles 29:12).

God doesn't have to share anything with us, but he does. Any good thing in your life comes from God! If you have enough food, clothes, toys, or clean water to share with others, you can remember what David prayed:

> *For all things come from you, and of your own have we given* *you. (1 Chronicles 29:14)*

When we remember that it all belongs to God and comes from God, it's easier to give some of it away. We're just borrowing it anyway.

What is something you have a hard time sharing? Write or draw about it. Then place your hand on what you wrote or drew and say, "It all comes from God and belongs to God." Does that help you hold it a little less tightly?

Mother's Prayer Section

Say to each other: Tell me about a promise
you've made to someone.

Have you ever been given a promise that you knew would be fulfilled only years later? Like "You can have a car when you turn 18," or "I'll take you for sushi when you get married." Those things feel like they're a very long time away when you're a kid!

Back when David first became king of Israel, God promised, "Your house and your kingdom shall be made sure forever before me. Your throne shall be established forever" (2 Samuel 7:16).

1 Chronicles 29 tells us that David was king for 40 years and finally died at age 70. His son Solomon took over as king, but he wasn't the one who would have this forever kingdom that God promised. We have to fast-forward a thousand years to find out who that was.

Matthew 1 tells us exactly how God fulfilled his promise, but he tells us through a list of names. Let's read the highlights:

David was the father of Solomon [this is followed by many more names of sons who had sons] and Jacob the father of Joseph the husband of Mary, of whom Jesus was born, who is called Christ. (Matthew 1:6–16)

You've heard of him, right? Jesus is the one who has the forever kingdom, just like we say at the end of the Lord's Prayer: "for Yours is the kingdom and the power and the glory, forever and ever."

Even though David wasn't perfect, he was like Jesus in a lot of ways.

- David saved a country of terrified people by going up against the bad guys by himself, which is like Jesus taking on the evil of the world by himself.

- David was the Shepherd King of Israel, and Jesus is the Shepherd King of the whole world.
- David tried his best to rule in justice and righteousness, and Jesus rules in perfect justice and righteousness.
- David trusted God even when hard things happened, and so did Jesus.
- When David did something amazing (like killing Goliath), he praised God and thanked God for his help. So did Jesus.

David never got to see God's promise fulfilled, but God definitely kept it. David was a God-chaser, and God is a promise-keeper. Aren't you glad God keeps his promises?

Write your mom's name and your name. This is part of another promise from God: "In the fear of the Lord [she] has strong confidence, and [her] children will have a refuge" (Proverbs 14:26). How do you feel knowing that you are part of an amazing promise from God too?

....

....

....

Mother's Prayer Section

....

....

....

....

Ask each other: What's something amazing that God created?

We know a lot about David's life from the stories in the Old Testament. But we know about David's love for God from the many psalms he wrote. We've looked at a few already, but we're going to look at a few more to help us learn about prayer.

Sometimes it feels like prayer is the easiest thing in the world, but other times we can think and think and think and still not know what to say.

Here's a simple trick that lots of Christians use to help them pray: they read Bible verses out loud! Bible verses from the Psalms can be especially helpful because most of them were already written as prayers. So we can use the words that David wrote to help us learn to pray. It's not cheating at all to use Bible verses when you pray!

What's the first thing to do when you don't know what to say? Look at God. I mean, don't look with your eyeballs. He's hard to see like that. But look around to see what God has done and what you know is true about God. Then tell him! That is called praising God.

In fact, we can use the word PRAY to remember how to pray! The first thing we do is the *P*: Praise God.

Let's look at an example of praise from Psalm 8. Praise is just telling God how awesome he is, so look at how David starts his prayer:

> *O Lord, our Lord,*
> *how majestic is your name in all the earth!*
> *You have set your glory above the heavens.*
>
> ....
>
> *When I look at your heavens, the work of your fingers,*

the moon and the stars, which you have set in place,
what is man that you are mindful of him,
and the son of man that you care for him?
(Psalm 8:1, 3–4)

Praise is about telling God how amazing he is! David said, "God, you are majestic," and "God, you made the heavens." That's praise.

When you look around, do you see God's amazing creation? He created the constellations in the sky and the soft smell of a new baby. He also created puffy clouds, bright colors, and sloppy dog kisses. There's a lot to praise him for, every day.

Let's practice! Finish these sentences: "God, you are…" and "God, you made…"

....

....

....

....

Mother's Prayer Section

....

....

....

....

Say to each other: Tell me about something you
did that hurt someone else this week.

Let's keep going through the four main parts of prayer! We can remember them through the letters of the word PRAY.

P: Praise

R: Repent

Remember what David did after he hurt Bathsheba and murdered Uriah? He turned away from his sin and chose to go God's way again. That's what repentance is: apologizing and turning away from sin.

Even though this happened 3,000 years ago, we know exactly what he said when he prayed because he wrote it down!

Have mercy on me, O God,
according to your steadfast love;

....

Against you, you only, have I sinned
and done what is evil in your sight.
(Psalm 51:1, 4)

Wait, what did that say? *Who* did David sin against? Didn't he sin against Bathsheba and Uriah? But he said to God, "Against you, you only, have I sinned."

When we sin, no matter who we hurt in the process, it also hurts God. So when we pray, it's important to apologize to God too. At first, it can feel weird saying, "Sorry, God, for hitting my brother," but it's so important!

In fact, did you know that apologizing to God is the first step to becoming a Christian?

We have all sinned. That's pretty obvious, right? I bet you have smacked someone, lied, or disobeyed your mom. We don't have to try hard to sin! It comes easily to us—like David and Adam and Eve and everyone else—because it's easier to disobey than to obey. And you know what all this disobedience does to our hearts? It makes them dirty. I don't mean your physical, blood-pumping heart is dirty. I'm talking about the part of you that connects with God. When your heart is dirty and gross, it keeps you from being in a good relationship with God.

David describes what God does for us like this:

Wash me, and I shall be whiter than snow.
(Psalm 51:7)

David asked God to clean his heart. Luckily for us, God had an ultimate plan to clean the hearts of everyone who wants it: Jesus. When we apologize to him, Jesus gives us something David called "a clean heart."

When you apologize to God, you'll feel joyful and peaceful because God will clean your heart too.

Let's practice! Finish this sentence: "God, I'm sorry for…" Then thank God for this promise from 1 John 1:9: "If we confess our sins, he is faithful and just to forgive us our sins and to cleanse us from all unrighteousness."

....

....

....

....

Mother's Prayer Section

Ask each other: What's something you want, right now?

Let's keep going through the four main parts of prayer! We can remember them through the letters of the word PRAY.

P: Praise

R: Repent

A: Ask

We have finally come to everyone's favorite part of prayer: asking. You've probably asked God for something before, right? Maybe you asked him for a baby brother, or a new bike, or a snow day, or a new video game system.

It's great to ask God for those things because he loves to hear from us, and those things are important to us. But sometimes we can start to think of God like a vending machine. You know the kind, right? You put in your money, push a few buttons, and a bag of snacks comes out the bottom. We sometimes think that if we say our prayers in the right way or behave nicely, then when we ask God for something he *has* to give it to us, like a vending machine has to give us our snacks. But he doesn't work that way!

Instead of asking for *things*, think of the Ask part of prayer as asking for *help* for yourself or someone else. Let's spy on one of David's asking prayers, and see if we can learn a bit about asking God for help.

Save me, O God!

For the waters have come up to my neck.

(Psalm 69:1)

David doesn't use any fancy words. He just tells God the problem and what he wants God to do: save him! He knows that God hears him, "For the Lord hears the needy and does not despise his own people who are prisoners" (Psalm 69:33).

We know that when we ask God for help, he will give it because he loves to help his beloved children. He doesn't always answer our prayers in the way we want, or when we want him to. The Bible says, "At an acceptable time, O God, in the abundance of your steadfast love answer me in your saving faithfulness" (Psalm 69:13). When we ask, we can also learn to tell God that we trust him to answer in whatever way he knows best because he loves us.

Draw a picture of someone who needs God's help right now.

Mother's Prayer Section

50 THE FOUR PARTS OF PRAY: YES

2 Samuel 15:25–26

Say to each other: Ask me a question you know I'll say yes to.

Let's keep going through the four main parts of prayer! We can remember them through the letters of the word PRAY.

P: Praise

R: Repent

A: Ask

Y: Yes

Finally, we come to the last part of PRAYing! We talked about praising God for who he is and what he's done. We talked about repenting, and about asking God for help.

Last, we need to learn to say yes. Prayer isn't just about talking to God; it's also about God talking to you and changing you. He wants to change you in amazing ways, making you more like Jesus. He wants to help you be strong and courageous, kind and generous, patient and joyful. But God won't change you if you don't want him to. You have to let him.

So after talking to God, there's a word we usually say. You might have even wondered what it means. It's the word *amen*, which means "so be it." When you say amen, you're basically saying, "I've told you what I need, but you do what you want to do. If you choose to do something else, so be it."

David said something just like this as he ran away from Jerusalem when Absalom tried to take over his kingdom:

> Then the king said to Zadok, "Carry the ark of God back into the city. If I find favor in the eyes of the Lord, he will bring me back and let me see both it and his dwelling place. But if he says, 'I have no pleasure in you,' behold, here I am, let him do to me what seems good to him." (2 Samuel 15:25–26)

David said yes to God. He said that God could do whatever he needed to do, and David would be OK with that. David would say yes to God's plan, no matter what it was, even if it meant never seeing the Ark of the Covenant again. If God chose not to let him come back to Jerusalem, so be it.

Saying yes to God can feel scary. Sometimes God asks us to do something that makes us feel uncomfortable. But he does everything out of love, and he promises to be with us to help us do hard things.

Are you ready to say yes to God? If so, write YES!

....

Mother's Prayer Section

....

....

....

....

....

....

....

....

Ask each other: What time of day do you normally pray?

If I told you there was a perfect time of day to pray, when do you think it would be? Here's a hint: it's not a time on a clock!

1 Thessalonians 5:17 says, "pray without ceasing." Uh-oh. Do you pray every second of your day? I don't either! But this verse doesn't mean that we should kneel down all day and all night and pray. We'd starve to death rather quickly. Rather, it means that we can talk to God all the time because he's always with us. Anytime we're ready, he's right there, ready to listen and respond.

Since we've been learning about prayer from the psalms of David, let's read a few more of them. I bet you'll find some more times to pray that you hadn't thought of before!

O Lord, in the morning you hear my voice;
in the morning I prepare a sacrifice for you and watch.
(Psalm 5:3)

OK, so we can pray in the morning. When else?

At midnight I rise to praise you,
because of your righteous rules.
(Psalm 119:62)

Have you ever prayed at midnight? What a great thing to do when you wake up from a bad dream: talk to God about it!

Here's another one—see if you can figure out what time of day it is.

My soul will be satisfied as with fat and rich food,
and my mouth will praise you with joyful lips,

when I remember you upon my bed,
and meditate on you in the watches of the night;
for you have been my help,
and in the shadow of your wings I will sing for joy.
(Psalm 63:5–7)

It sounds like David had trouble sleeping and remembered that he could praise God all night instead of tossing and turning. But just in case you think you can pray only in the morning or at night, here's one more:

Evening and morning and at noon
I utter my complaint and moan,
and he hears my voice.
(Psalm 55:17)

Evening and morning and noon! There's no time of day that's off-limits for prayer.

Are you riding your bike? Talk to God.

Are you taking a shower? Talk to God.

Are you taking a test? Talk to God.

Are you playing sports? Talk to God.

What other times of day can you think of? Draw or write them here!

Mother's Prayer Section

Ask each other: What do you do with
your body when you pray?

Did you know that you don't have to pray with your hands folded and your eyes closed? That's not even in the Bible! We pray like that because it helps us concentrate, but there are many different ways to pray. Some of them come from David's psalms.

Many of the Old Testament leaders prayed with their arms outstretched. Moses, Solomon, David, and Jeremiah all talk about praying with arms up. Psalm 63:4 says,

> *So I will bless you as long as I live;*
> *in your name I will lift up my hands.*

Stop right now and test out that position. How does it make you feel? What kind of prayers do you want to pray when your arms are up like that?

Another way people prayed in the Bible was on their knees. Psalm 95:6 says,

> *Oh come, let us worship and bow down;*
> *let us kneel before the Lord, our Maker!*

Stop right now and kneel on the floor, putting your forehead on the floor like you're bowing to a king. How does it make you feel? What kind of prayers do you want to pray when you are bowing down before God? Psalm 63:5–6 says,

> *My soul will be satisfied as with fat and rich food,*
> *and my mouth will praise you with joyful lips,*
> *when I remember you upon my bed,*
> *and meditate on you in the watches of the night.*

What kind of position are you in when you're on your bed? Test out that position right now! What kind of prayers do you want to pray when you are lying down?

There are so many other ways to use your body to pray, and you have your whole life to try them out!

Now that you know how to be a God-chaser, I hope you'll continue to chase God all your life.

May you be great like David, full of the Holy Spirit, brave and courageous, full of trust in God, unashamed to follow and worship God, and repentant when you do wrong. And may God bless you like he blessed David, giving you his presence, his Spirit, and his courage, love, and power.

What is something you most want to remember from the past 52 days with David? Instead of writing it down, go into one of the prayer positions we talked about today and tell God.

Mother's Prayer Section

ACKNOWLEDGMENTS

I want to dedicate this book to Ethan, Oliver, and Jackson, without whom I could not have written this mother and son prayer journal. Your honesty, curiosity, and creativity forced me to dig deeper and give it everything I had. And, of course, I wouldn't even have my sweet boys without my amazing husband, Jonathon, nor would I actually have had time to write. So thank you for picking up the slack when I was too distracted by the thoughts in my brain to keep track of our home and family.

A huge thanks goes out to the fellow boy moms who helped me uncover the theme and structure of this book: Mindy Britt, Tara Cole, Melanie Ross, and Kristin Vanderlip. After uncovering the theme and structure, my amazing critique partners helped me chisel off the dirt and find the gems underneath. Thanks to Bethany Den Boer, Belinda Grimbeek, Laura Ann Miller, Nicole Schrader, and Susan Simpson for your encouragement and useful criticism.

At the beginning of his compositions, Bach often wrote "JJ," which stood for the Latin phrase "Jesu juva." It means "Jesus, help." That was my prayer at the beginning, middle, and end of this book. At the end of his compositions, he wrote "SDG," which stood for "Soli Deo gloria," for God's glory alone. These are my first and final acknowledgments. Thank you, Jesus, for your help, now and always.

Soli Deo gloria.

ABOUT THE AUTHOR

Christie Thomas lives in Alberta, Canada, and is mom to three amazing boys. She is the author of *Quinn's Promise Rock* and *Quinn Says Goodbye,* and loves to help Christian moms nurture deep faith roots in their kids through her online work at littleshootsdeeproots. com. Her favorite thing to do with her boys is read good stories and do wacky science experiments.